William Thorn Warren

St. Cross Hospital Near Winchester

It's History and Buildings

William Thorn Warren

St. Cross Hospital Near Winchester
It's History and Buildings

ISBN/EAN: 9783744689823

Printed in Europe, USA, Canada, Australia, Japan

Cover: Foto ©ninafisch / pixelio.de

More available books at **www.hansebooks.com**

St. Cross Hospital

near Winchester:

Its History and Buildings.

SIXTY ILLUSTRATIONS.

EDITED BY

WILLIAM THORN WARREN,

(For two years an ex-officio Trustee of the Hospital).

PREFACE.

As all the works treating solely of the Hospital of St. Cross have been out of print for some time past, I have been asked to prepare this small Handbook. In its hasty compilation I have endeavoured to locate the charm of its adventitious history by accompanying the notes with carefully selected illustrations: for many of these I am indebted to the great patience and skill of the photographer, Mr. W. T. Green.

St. Cross is one of the earliest foundations for the care of impotent men,—a sort of mediæval convalescent home,— the noble Founder's idea being that the best medicine for enfeebled health is a generous diet, coupled with a regular and peaceful life. For the "hundred-hall" poor, who did not need medical treatment, coarser bread and only one dish was allowed.

In placing this book before the public, I wish to acknowledge the assistance I have received from the Master and Brothers of St. Cross, the representatives of the late Canon Humbert, from Messrs. Macmillan and Co., from Papers by Professor Freeman, B. W. Greenfield, F.S.A., Rev. J. G. Joyce, F.S.A., Rev. Dr. Fearon, Woodward's "Hampshire," Duthy's "Sketches," a synoptical Letter to the "Times," April, 1896, and from various writers on St. Cross to whose works reference is made.

W. T. W.

Winchester,
   November, 1899.

CONTENTS.

———

List of Illustrations.

BISHOP HENRY DE BLOIS' TREASURY IN WINCHESTER CATHEDRAL.

EAST SIDE OF OUTER COURT, ST. CROSS.

MR. LECKY ON THE VALUE OF THE HISTORY OF LOCAL INSTITUTIONS.

" I would especially commend to the attention of all political students the history of institutions in the constantly fluctuating conditions of human life. No institution has ever remained for a long period unaltered. Sometimes with changed beliefs and changed conditions, institutions lose all their original utility. They become simply useless, obstructive, and corrupt; and, though by mere passive resistance they may continue to exist long after they have ceased to serve any good purpose, they will at last be undermined by their own abuses. Other institutions, on the other hand, show that true characteristic of vitality, the power of adapting themselves to changed conditions and new utilities. Few things in history are more interesting and more instructive than a careful study of these transformations. There is probably no better test of the political genius of a nation than the power which it possesses of adapting old institutions to new wants; and it is in this skill and in this disposition that the political pre-eminence of the English people has been most conspicuously shown." [1]

[1] An Inaugural Address reported in *The Times*, October 11, 1892.

THE MASTER OF ST. CROSS.

(Hon. and Rev. Canon Brodrick M. A.)

Notes on the Hospital of St. Cross.

(Founded A.D. 1136.)

There is a power in Imagination which enables us seemingly to enter into the very bodily presence of men long since gathered to the dust.— RUSKIN.

ORE than seven centuries have passed since Bishop Henry de Blois, the Founder of St. Cross Hospital, watched his builders puddle the clay for the foundations of his houses "for the poor of Christ," and saw them rear the lofty chancel and transepts of his great church. He lived twenty years after this at Wolvesey Castle, situate a little higher up stream. The first Brothers of St. Cross doubtless saw his art treasures, and the fine collection of wild beasts and birds which he kept there, and they would also see the piece of land, where once stood the Conqueror's palace, which their Founder was laying

B

out and adding to the minster precincts. They probably viewed with some curiosity the Byzantine Font which he had brought from abroad, and praised the beauty of the new treasury and shrines which he was erecting in the Cathedral.

When only twenty-eight years old, Henry de Blois was made bishop, but having become infirm after some forty years of political and episcopal life in the troublous times of Stephen, he would occupy himself by seeing his Brethren (dressed as now) and his Hundred-hall Poor eating their *mortrell*[1] of *wastell*[2] and milk, or barley bread with "green fish" or herring pie (and sometimes " plum broth," " honey sop," or a farthing's worth of cheese), and quaffing their *galiones* of small beer from " horns " and leathern "jacks."

Soon after the Founder's death, a dispute arose between the Bishop and the Hospitallers, (to whom the management of the Hospital had been entrusted,) but after the lapse of many years the Hospital was handed over to the sole charge of Bishop Peter de Rupibus, who appointed Alan de Soke, "a prudent and faithful man," as the first Master.

The west end of the church remaining unfinished in 1255 Bp. Ethelmar invited assistance towards its completion, and he appears to have been successful without the aid of the modern bazaar or sale of work.

In 1345, the "bell-ropes," together with a missal

[1] basin.   [2] best bread.

and a chalice, were delivered into the hands of Master
Raymund de Pelegrini at his induction. In 1350 the
Master was paid £8, and the four priests 13s. 4d. each
per year ; the seven choristers lived on the leavings
of the Master and Brethren, and the Hundred-hall
Poor were allowed to carry home with them what
they did not consume of their dinner, which consisted
of three quarts of small beer, a loaf of bread, and two
messes.

In 1321, Bp. Reginald Asser, and again in 1372,
Bp. William of Wykeham, had to wrest the property
of the Hospital from the spoiler. In the latter case
one Master, de Cloune, sold the corn, cattle, and
materials, pulled down buildings, allowed the roof of
the Great Hall to remain fallen in, and turned away
the Brethren and Hundred-hall Poor!

Towards the end of the fourteenth century, that
worthy Master, John de Campeden, expended £1,822,
a sum now equal to about £27,000, on the repair of
the Hospital buildings.

In 1446, Cardinal Beaufort added a new foundation,
or Alms-house of Noble Poverty, for thirty-five new
Brothers and three Hospital Nurses, raising the
number of inmates to seventy. . . . . .

One wonders if the great Cardinal invited the
Brothers of Noble Poverty to Wolvesey to see the
regal crown which he held in pawn for the large loan
he had granted to the King. No doubt they heard
the Cardinal preach at the rededication of their church

in 1420, for he was an eloquent man, as is known by the record of his speeches delivered in Parliament.

At the Reformation the Vicar General found "certain things requiring reformation," and ordered that refreshment but *no money* be given to honest people . . . . mendicants were to be driven away with staves. The Lord's Prayer and the Creed were to be taught *in English*, and to be said in the Church after dinner. The choral services were allowed to be continued.

In 1632, in answer to Archbishop Laud's inquiry, the Master reported that he found the Hospital buildings in "extreme ruin and dilapidation."

During Cromwell's protectorate, the regicides Lisle and Cook (solicitor to the Parliament) were Masters of the Hospital successively; and in 1667 the office was filled by the soldier-priest, Henry Compton, who afterwards as Bishop of London crowned William and Mary.

The ancient Registers of the Hospital were burnt in 1616, and Bishop Hoadly in 1763 granted a licence to pull down the Ambulatory, which happily was not done, so that to-day visitors can view the buildings much as they appeared four hundred years ago.

The Hospital Buildings consist of an Outer Gate and Court, in which, on the left, are the brewhouse and remains of some of the earlier buildings; on the right, the large kitchen, offices, etc. Under the Tower, which is a restoration by Cardinal Beaufort, worthy of his name, is the Porter's hatchway, from whence the far-famed Dole of a piece of bread and small horn of beer is given to all wayfarers.

Passing from the fore-court through the noble tower gateway, one enters upon the spacious quadrangle around which are ranged the Brethren's Hall,[1] the Master's House, the quaint dwellings of the Brethren, the lofty Church ; on the east side the Infirmary with Ambulatory beneath, and on the south the Home Park and Burial Ground of the Society.

East of the Ambulatory is the Master's garden with its ancient fish pond and remains of a great pigeon-house.

All readers will be charmed by the short record of a visit to the Hospital by an American lady, which we take from her delightful little volume, with the kind permission of the publishers, Messrs. Macmillan & Co., of London and New York.

The Brothers with courtesy take visitors "the rounds."

---

[1] There are at the present time seventeen brothers in all, and our illustration of the entrance to the Hall shews the Brother for the day giving seventeen rings for dinner—one for each Brother—to fetch his rations.

RECEIVING THE DOLE.

THE BRETHREN'S HOUSES.

A Visit to St. Cross Hospital by an American Lady.

We entered in under a fine vaulted gateway with a square turret above it, and found ourselves in a small court, on one side of which was the porter's lodge. A tall, slender, gentle-eyed woman, with a little boy clinging to her skirts, responded to our knock by opening the upper half of the door. We paid our sixpences, and were about to pass on when she said, with a smile, "Will you have your dole *now*, or when you have been the rounds?" . . . . .

"We will have it now, if you please," we said gravely. Whereupon the portress opened the lower half of the door with a hospitable air, and bade us enter. We looked round for our dole expectantly. From an urn-shaped vessel placed in a niche in the wall the portress filled two drinking-cups—horn, bound with silver—with pale, amber-coloured beer, and presented them to us with bits of bread about two inches square. "The poor get a whole slice," she said, consolingly. The beer was not so bad as to flavour that day, but it was certainly amazingly weak. The "Wayfarer's Dole" is said to be the last known survival of the good old custom of offering food to all chance comers. We felt as if

we had gone back seven centuries, notwithstanding the
assurance that the Prince of Wales had drunk from that
very cup only the week before.

Then we passed into the large quadrangle, and paused
to look about us.   In front of us was a beautiful gray
church : to the east an old cloister ; to the right, forming
two sides of the square, a row of curious low, white houses,
with very tall chimneys, connected with a longer building
of the same height, but with a broad arched doorway and
an imposing flight of steps.   Each little house had its own
little garden, gay with flowers.   Around the great green
quadrangle ran a broad gravelled walk.   In its centre was
an old sun-dial on a gray, time-eaten pedestal.   As we
looked, still standing near the gate, a gentle-faced old man
in a black gown, with a silver cross on his breast, came
slowly across the square looking at us inquiringly.   There
was an air of almost infantile sweetness and simplicity about
him, an atmosphere of unworldliness, so to speak, that
captivated us at once.   In a timorous, hesitating way he
half extended his hand in welcome, and then half withdrew
it again ; and when we cordially gave him ours, begging him
to show us the beautiful old place, he beamed and
brightened, stepping off bravely as he led us from point to
point, babbling delightedly like a happy child. . . . . His
placid face seemed to be part of the scene and to belong
to it.   What to him was the fever and tumult of the life
outside ? what the surging thunder of the waves that he
only heard in the far distance ? what the mad whirl of the
rushing, swarming, scheming, bargaining, fighting multi-
tudes ? What had his own past been ? Whatever it was, he
had forgotten it, with its pains and its conflicts.   For him
there remained, until the day of his death, only an infinite
peace. . . . . .   There was a lump in my throat, and a very
suspicious aching, as we followed him from church to

BROTHER BARTHOLOMEW'S PORTRAIT.

cloister, and from thence across the court to the "Hundred
Mennes Hall," where the brethren still dine together on
state occasions, or "gaudy days" as our guide called them.

THE ROSTER.

Here the old, blackened
roof-timbers still remain; here
is the gallery from which grace
was said and the benediction
given, and where often the
minstrels sang and the harpers
played in the old days of
knights and troubadours; here
is the daïs at the east for the
high officials, with the humbler
tables of the brothers ranged
along the sides; and here is
the old raised hearth in the
centre of the hall, clouded by
the smoke of centuries. Here
are the black leathern "Jacks,"
or jugs, wherein the beer once
foamed, and (safely shrined
behind glass doors), the salt-
cellars and candlesticks of the
great Cardinal Beaufort him-
self. You may sit in his chair if you please, and fancy
yourself Lord Bishop of Winchester!

In the kitchen our gentle old guide showed us the
great tables where the "joints" are carved. "We choose
for the best cuts," he said, "taking our turns in order.
See!" and he laughed gleefully as he pointed to a list of
names fastened to the wall. "It will be my turn to-morrow,
for I am brother Comas. That's my name—the third one."

As we came out into the quadrangle again he hesitated
a moment. "Would you like to see how the Brethren

live?" he asked. "Would it please you to see my rooms?"
. . . . "Here's where I live," he said, with a charming air
of proprietorship. "We're very comfortable. There's no
choice here. The houses are all alike." There was a
sitting-room, or parlour, with a bright little latticed window
and a fireplace, a bedroom with a neat white bed, and a
tiny kitchen, or buttery, with a sink and running water. A
little round table was drawn up before the fire, and the
cloth was laid, with a pretty teacup and saucer and sundry
other dishes. Brother Comas had evidently been about to
make his own tea when our approach interrupted the
ceremony. "Now you must see my garden and have some
flowers."

*   *   *   *   *   *

But we carried away with us something better than
flowers the memory of a beautiful charity, and a picture
of lovely, serene old age whose colours will never fade.
Good-bye, dear old Brother Comas![1]

[1] *A Cathedral Pilgrimage*, by Julia C. R. Dorr, Macmillan, 2s. 6d.

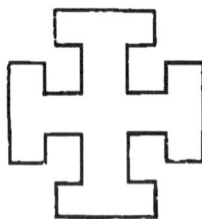

SILVER CROSS WORN BY THE BROTHERS ON THE LEFT BREAST.

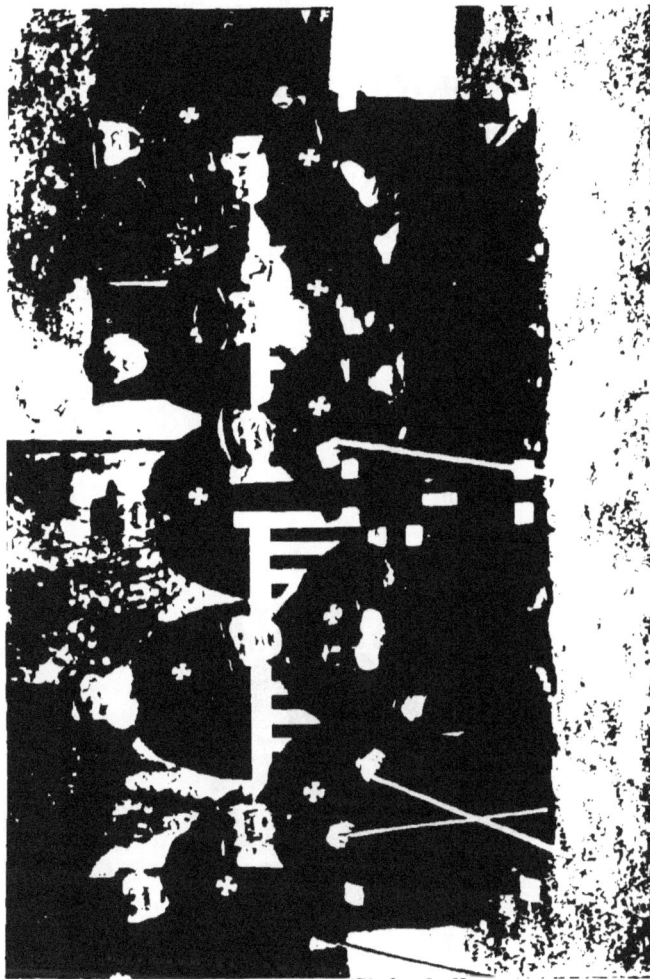

T. Mondey.   H. J. Rogers.   R. Dicker.   G. Boyce.   H. Fevercourt.

T. Noyce.   W. Brothwell.   J. Wells.   A. Noble.   C. Dale.

SOME OF THE BROTHERS OF DE BLOIS FOUNDATION, SEPTEMBER, 1899.

(Three Brothers were absent.)

The Hospital Buildings.

"St. Cross is the most famous and most ancient of existing eleemosynary institutions."

The Outer Court.

IN the Outer Court, on the left, are remains of an ancient building about 40ft. long, probably a portion of the earlier buildings of St. Cross Hospital ; and on the right the large kitchen, offices, etc.

The wandering friars in mediæval times were the newsmen of the day, and important commissions and valuable parcels were often committed to them. At night some of the belated wayfarers were probably allowed to sleep in some of the domestic buildings in the outer Court.

CROWN OF THORNS.

The centre boss of the groining of the gateway is a curious cross composed of leaves, surrounded by a crown of thorns. In the spandrels over the gate appear the Founder's arms, France and England quarterly, within a border.

Wilson, Photo.

THE MASTER'S HOUSE.   HALL.   BEAUFORT'S TOWER.   AMBULATORY.

The Cloister, or Ambulatory.

On the east is a low Cloister of the 16th century,
135ft. in length, almost domestic in style, with oriel
window and simple spandrels to the supporting
woodwork. One part of the building affords an early
specimen of brickwork, some of the bricks being of
small make. One of the nun's rooms in the upper
part of the Cloister opens into the Church, where
was formerly a gallery whereby the sick in the
Infirmary had an opportunity of taking part in the
services. The solid oval table in the lower walk is
said to have been brought from Winchester Castle.
Near by is the entrance to the Master's garden, where
still remain the old fish pond, and the walls of a
great pigeon house.

On the west side are the Brethren's Houses, with
their tall, quaint chimneys,[1] and on the north side are
the Refectory and the Master's House.

Beaufort Tower.

Beaufort Tower (1404–47) rises above the roofing
on either side, and its outline is relieved by a handsome octagonal turret with spiral stair. The vault of
the gateway is richly groined, and over it is the
Founder's Chamber, or muniment room. The niche
in the south exterior was formerly occupied by a

---

[1] These chimneys were probably added at the time of the enlargement
of the Hospital by Cardinal Beaufort about the year 1420. In the Brothers'
Hall the central hearth for a charcoal fire, with an opening in the roof
above, was allowed to remain. A chimney in Founder's chamber over the
gateway was constructed in 1392-3.

THE AMBULATORY.

C

figure of the Blessed Virgin, which fell nearly a
century ago, almost crushing one of the brethren in
its fall. This statue had been preserved from destruc-
tion by iconoclasts, through an invented story that
it represented a milkmaid with a pail on her head.
On the north side the only remaining figure in the
three niches is that of the Cardinal in a kneeling
posture. The central niche was probably occupied
by a figure of the Blessed Virgin, and the other by a
figure of the Angel Gabriel,[1] in accordance with the
dedication of the Cardinal's Chantry Chapel in the
Cathedral. On the southern face is a vertical sundial.

L'Estrange says :—" In the cornice on the tower over
the archway are four heads —those of Henry IV, 'time-
honoured' Lancaster, Beaufort, and Catherine Swinford.
Catherine here finds herself in good company. She was,
as most know, a pretty governess whom John of Gaunt's
wife had the temerity to engage, with the result that her
husband had several natural children, [afterwards legiti-
mated], among them Cardinal Beaufort. Over these heads
are the canopied niches for statues, the idea being evidently
taken from those on the College tower. In the centre was
the Virgin, and by her side the Cardinal ; but we observe
that though he is on his knees, he is too grand to take off
his hat to her." [2]

The Trustees meet in the Founder's chamber over
the gateway, and there the ancient documents are
kept.

[1] Some writers say that this niche was filled with a figure representing
Bishop de Blois, the first founder.

[2] *Royal Winchester*, p. 247.

THE COURTYARD.

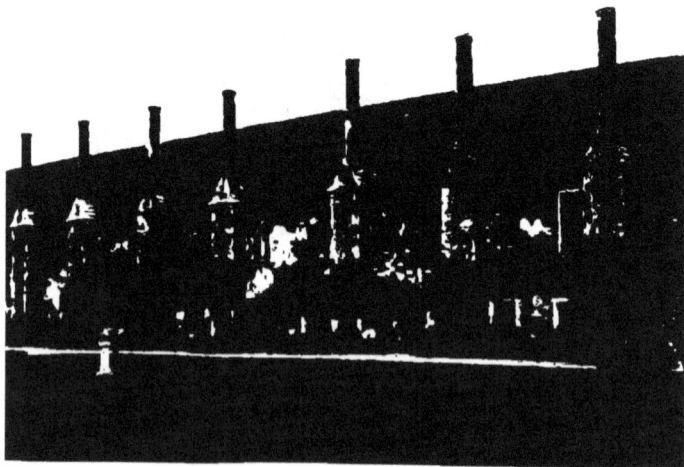

HOUSES OF THE BRETHREN.

The Houses of the Brothers.

The existing Brethren's houses, like those of the Carthusians, have two rooms, a pantry, and garden. The tall chimneys are usually attributed to Cardinal Beaufort (1420). The ancient Lock Burn crosses under the outer court, and runs at the back of the brothers' houses, whence it turns southward towards the river. A yearly rent is paid to the Cathedral estate for the use of this rivulet.

The dress of the Brothers, derived from the Hospitallers, is a long black gown with a silver cross on the left breast.

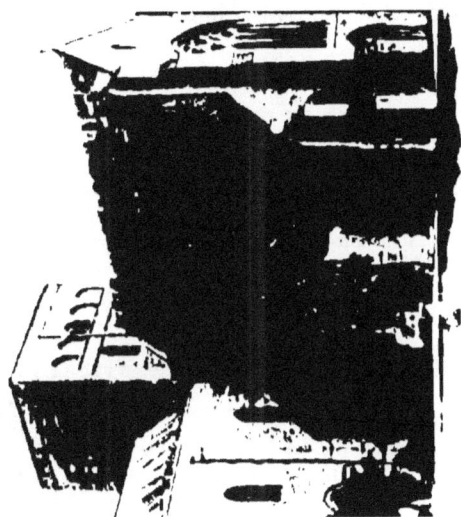

Approximate Dates of the Church

as gathered from the Architecture by Brother Lewin.

	A.D.
Sacristy	1130
Lower part of North and South Transepts ...	1130–1170
Chancel	1135–1189
North Aisle East	1170–1200
South Aisle East	1170–1220
Nave	
First Bay	1170–1190
Second Bay	1220–1240
North Aisle ... ... 1170 to	1230–1240
South Aisle	1170–1230
Triforium from Boss	1220–1240
and the Four Westerly Arches	1245
West End of Aisle and South Door	1200–1220
West End of North Aisle and Porch... ...	1200–1240
West Door	1240
West Window	1230–1240
Clerestory	1255
Two Windows South Side	1325
Groining, Transepts	1170–1200
Tower raised	1380–1410
Church Finished The Lantern and Bell Chamber: Window inserted in Early English	1255

Dates of Styles of Architecture.

	Introduced	Lasted
Saxon	950–1066	116
Norman	1066–1170	104
Transition ...	1170–1200	30
Early English ...	1200–1240	40
Late English ...	1240–1270	30
Geometric or Early Decorated }	1270–1330	60
Flowing	1330–1380	50
Perpendicular ...	1380–1485	105
Tudor	1485–1546	61
Renaissance ...	1546–1650	104
Debased	1650–1840	190
		890

SOUTH-EAST VIEW OF INTERIOR, BEFORE RESTORATION.

The Church.

"The Church, celebrated throughout England for its later Norman choir, still with its stately outline 'crowns the watery glade.'"—*The Times*.

Dimensions of the Church.

Extreme length, W. to E. ...	... 125 feet
,, breadth at Transepts	... 115 ,,
Nave and Aisle, breadth of ...	... 54 ,,
Nave, height of	... 57 ,,
Tower Lantern, inside height of	... 77 ,,

SQUINCH.

ANGLE OF TOWER.

The Church (1771–1292) is one of the most interesting architectural studies. Good examples of every style— from Romanesque, Transition-Norman, and Early English to Late Decorated— are seen here. In Transition-Norman this Church is considered the best example in existence. Its height is good, and it has stone vaulting throughout.

The Church remained thatched with straw till A.D. 1334, when William de Edyndon, master, re-roofed the Nave with lead, erected the windows of the clerestory, built a chamber for the Master, and re-roofed the "Hundred Mennes Hall."

The Church was re-dedicated on the Saturday in the second week of October, 1420. After the ceremony, the

THE WEST FRONT.

Warden gave a dinner in the College Hall to some friends,
including Boreway, Keswyck, Kyngesmylle, Pyes, Smythford,
Welman, and *three people from the village of St. Cross.
Four singing men from St. Cross*, and Deverose, "the
litigious tailor," dined with the servants on this occasion.
Fromond, the steward, Keswyck, and Tychfeld, were guests
at supper.[1]

A.D. 1382–1410. John de Campeden, Master, completed the present tower, re-roofed the chancel and aisles,
etc., and expended a sum nearly equivalent to £27,000.

The West Front.

The doorway with the splendid west window, the
graceful lancets at the ends of the aisles, and the small gable
lights, all form one of the most beautiful and simple com-
positions imaginable.[2]

The splendid geometrical tracery in the great western
window is "fully developed Decorated."

The workmanship of the western Early English doorway
is excellent, and presents a good variety of tooth ornament.

Notes on the Exterior.

Woodward thinks it probable, from the dimensions of
the Transepts, and the squeezed appearance of the lower
east window of the North Transept, that the body of the
Church has been widened subsequently to its first erection
by Bishop Henry de Blois. The buttresses on the south
of Nave are of three styles.

[1] Kirby's *Annals of Winchester College*, p. 179.
[2] Freeman.

DOORWAY—NORTH OF CHANCEL.

In the south-east corner of the South Transept is a "Triple-arch." Probably it was a doorway, and led to some small cloister leading to a small building—perhaps the "Clerken-house" pulled down by Cloune, the habitation of the seven choristers and their schoolmaster, a portion of the Nave wall being cut away in order that the door might open right in the angle for some interior convenience.

The vast thickness of the walls in Norman Churches made the use of buttresses less necessary ; thus only tall, shallow pilasters are found adjacent to Norman work.

The parapets are a later addition.

In the south aisle the first window from the east is Norman, the second partly Early English, and the third pure Early English.

The upper windows in the Choir and Transepts are of later date than the lower. In early times builders did not usually "adopt" a style, but used or improved the style of their day; thus it is that the date of their work can generally be traced.

The nail head moulding, on the round windows in the eastern gable, was a first development of the tooth ornament. These openings (now glazed), were made to admit air to the roof timbers.

Even this fine church has a show side. The cloisters and domestic buildings were on the south, and the north side being more open, was more richly decorated, especially the windows, which on the south side are plain.

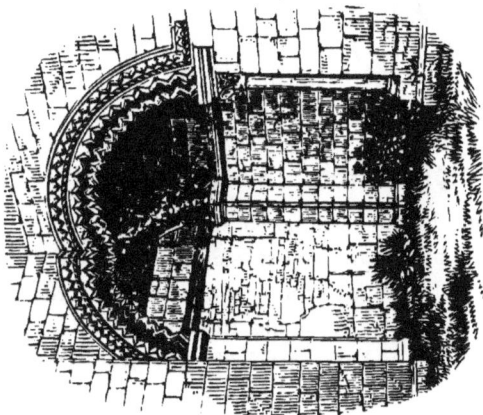

TRIPLE ARCH. INTERIOR.

TRIPLE ARCH EXTERIOR.

TURRET AT EAST END.

The north porch is Early English; note the room above with the elegant little window.

In the Nave, the windows vary from Transition - Norman to Early English, and in the clerestory, become Decorated. The windows in the north side are the richest.

The walls and windows of the Choir Aisles are Late Norman. At the end of the Church are square towers rising from flat buttresses.

View from the West End.

Entering by the north porch, the visitor is impressed by the indescribable charm and substantial dignity of this lofty Church, which is vaulted throughout. The lantern, formed out of the lower storey of the arcaded central tower, is a striking feature, and the enriched early Norman work at the east end, with interlacing arches and exquisitely carved window mouldings, viewed from the west end (a distance of 125 feet), having in the foreground the large circular columns, forms a graceful picture long to be remembered.

WINDOW NORTH AISLE.

The Nave.

Some twenty feet above the floor level may be noticed
sticking out from the piers of the tower-arch next the nave,
the two ends of the timbers of the rood-loft, which was
taken down by simply sawing through the beam.

BASES OF COLUMNS IN NAVE.

Every ornamental feature of the Norman style may be
seen in the interior of this Church.

The western portion of the Church, and the west
window were erected during the Mastership of Peter de
Sancto Mario, (A.D. 1289,) whose canopied tomb is a con-
spicuous feature on the north side of the Nave.

The groined roof of Nave is of the Decorated period.

The Norman string course ends after the first Nave
arch next to the Tower, and a bunch of foliage denotes
where the Early English work follows on.

Some of the windows have steps within the sill, which
in the south aisle serves to distinguish the shortness of the
part actually pierced for light.

INTERIOR OF CHURCH—LOOKING WEST.

The upper windows of the north transept are pointed, while in the south transept they are still round-headed.

A plain string course runs round the *older* part of the church, level with the window sills.

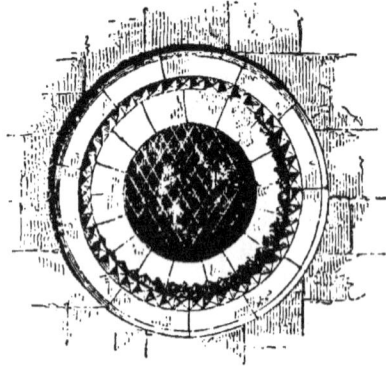

WINDOW IN EAST GABLE.

Notes on the Interior.

The interior of the Church, which deserves careful notice in all its details, is remarkable for the loftiness of its proportions and the rich ornamentation of its arches and mouldings. It has been restored and colored. The simplicity of the vaulted ceiling and the grandeur of the columns should be noticed.

BASE OF COLUMN IN NAVE.

The western portion of the Nave is Early English; the bay next the Transepts is Transition-Norman; the east end is Norman.

EAST WINDOW OF NORTH TRANSEPT.

The bird's beak moulding (developed into full-winged birds) is worthy of notice.

The Tower.

The whole Tower was, in the opinion of Mr. Freeman, open to the interior of the Church, and the run of the upper arches formed a sort of open gallery or outer triforium.

The eight perpendicular windows in the Tower are the work of John de Campeden (1390). He also paved the Church throughout.

The corbel heads which support the " solar " floor of the lantern are very boldly designed.

Beautiful Fourteenth Century Tiles.

On the north, outside the Chancel, is an interesting sedilia and bracket.— Note the carving.

The encaustic tiles bearing the appropriate motto for a house of prayer, "HAVE MYNDE," probably date from 1390. The new tiles are from

SEDILIA AND BRACKET. the old designs. The letters Z. O. refer to the anonymous contributor to the recent restorations.

All the old tiles have been re-laid, with due regard to pattern, in the North and South Aisles. They rest upon a pavement of York stone, beneath which there is complete ventilation. The Nave and Choir are laid with Minton's new tiles from old designs. In some the initials of the benefactor, Z. O., are shown.

Some similar examples of these early encaustic tiles may also be seen in Winchester Cathedral, Netley Abbey,

Photo. by Stuart, Southampton   INTERIOR OF CHURCH—LOOKING EAST.

Beaulieu Abbey, Romsey, Christchurch, Sopley, and Nurs-
ling Churches. Probably they were made at a kiln at
Poole or Romsey.

Tile 4 on the sheet of illustrations is an eagle having
two heads, typifying a rule that claimed to extend over both
the eastern and western empires. The German Emperors
adopted the double-headed eagle for their heraldic ensign
in support of their claim to be the successors of the Roman
Cæsars. This interesting encaustic tile probably relates to
and commemorates Richard, King of the Romans, Earl
of Cornwall and Poitou, younger brother of our King
Henry III, who adopted this eagle, bearing on its breast
a shield charged with a lion rampant crowned. Richard
was a liberal benefactor to the Abbey of Beaulieu, on the
Southampton Water, which had been founded by King
John in 1204.

Design No. 6 represents monkeys rampant and com-
batant with tails erect and in base, and between the feet
of the monkeys a fleur-de-lys. It is interesting to note that
the armorial bearings of the ancient family of St. John of
Basing include two monkey supporters.

Design No. 26 represents part of a rose or wheel-
window in Decorated style.

The other designs include the lion (9), [similar in
design to the lion's head on the Sanctuary door at
Durham Cathedral] the emblem of the Redeemer; the
dragon (11 and 13), the emblem of sin; the symbols of
the Cross (19 and 28); the dove (24), the emblem of
peace; the lily or fleur-de-lys (6 and 7), the emblem of
purity.

Specimens of Fourteenth Century Til

the Church of St. Cross, Winchester.

PERPENDICULAR CHANCEL SCREEN.

The earliest make of tile is that in which the pattern was first stamped in, then filled in with a different coloured clay, and afterwards covered with a transparent glaze. These tiles did not come into use until the end of the twelfth century.[1]

Cbe Chancel and Choir.

Early rude and later delicate Norman carving can both be observed in the Choir.

In the Choir the pointed arch is used throughout as an arch of construction, but the semi-circular arch is retained as an arch of decoration.

Above the pier arches of the Choir is the celebrated triforium of intersecting arches.

The Choir, like that at Romsey, is enclosed by a stone wall.

The elaborate Perpendicular Screen, which divides the Chancel from the North Choir Aisle, was brought from the demolished Church of St. Faith.

The very beautiful Renaissance carving in the Chancel is of about the period of Henry VII. The arrangement of the windows in the east end is very effective.

At the base of the present Communion Table is placed John de Campeden's (1382) original Purbeck Altar Slab, with its five consecration crosses, in good preservation.

John de Campeden's fine floor brass (1382) lies within the Chancel rails.

On one of the Choir Stalls is carved the name of one of the singing men, with the date 1572, shewing that the choral service survived the time of Henry VIII.

[1] See Paper by B. W. Greenfield, F.S.A., *Hants Field Club Proceedings*, vol. ii, p. 141.

THE NORTH TRANSEPT.

The lower window on the right was formerly a folding shutter, which opened from the Infirmary to a gallery from which the sick could hear the Service.

The orientation of the Church, like that of the Cathedral and College Chapel, is a little south of the true east.

The eagle and scroll on the small credence table doubtless refer to the Hospitallers of St. John, who were appointed by Bp. Henry de Blois administrators of the charity.

The Ancient Sacristy.

The ancient sacristy is entered from the south transept. It has a vaulted roof, and there are three recesses or aumbries for keeping the sacred vessels. From the outside it can be seen that the roof has been twice lowered.

THE ANCIENT SACRISTY (A.D. 1130).
Adjoining South Transept.

The vault has cross springers, and the room is lighted by a small loop window. The adjoining chamber appears to be of more recent date. The string course on the outside of the southern side of the Choir is quite flat on the under surface, having had the roof of a cloister underneath it.

ANCIENT LECTERN, WITH PARROT'S HEAD.

The Transepts.

In the transepts can best be seen the gradual change from Norman to Early English in the lancet-shaped windows.

The north chancel pier was found to contain a central Purbeck column cased circularly with Caen stone, this again octagonally cased with perpendicular work (see illustration of Interior before Restoration). The outer casing has been removed. The corresponding column on the south has no central Purbeck column. The octagonal outer casing must have been added by John de Campeden to gain increased strength.

Two fragments of a border, now placed in one of the North Transept windows, are considered by Winston to be the earliest glass in the neighbourhood, and to have come out of one of the Norman windows.

In the South Transept once stood an altar to St. Thomas of Canterbury. In the back of a recess over the site of the altar are remains of a painting representing the murder of Thomas à Becket —some Norman knights, a priest interposing, but not the prostrate archbishop can be traced.

On the south wall of the South Transept is a fresco of the Descent from the Cross, covering the whole of the wall ; very indistinct. Not only can a portion of the representation of the Saviour be seen, but, amongst other things, the tops of the houses at Jerusalem. This wall painting could be seen from the upper cloister room which opened into the Church.

In the South Transept are curious brackets supporting the clustered vaulting shafts.

Ltd.

NORTH AISLE—LOOKING EAST.

Triforium.

All around the Choir there is a second triforium, or passage, beneath the windows of the clerestory. At the end of the fourteenth century the Choir roofs were so lowered that the small pointed triforium windows, which were glazed in 1378, can be seen outside.

THE TRIFORIUM—SOUTH TRANSEPT.

The Aisles.

The sites of original altars may be seen at the ends of both the choir aisles, and at the east wall of the south transept. These and others were probably destroyed by order of Archbishop Laud.

In the North Aisle of Choir remains of ancient wall painting may be traced on both sides at the east end and on vaulting.

MORNING CHAPEL—SOUTH AISLE.

In these Aisles can be seen the chevron, the billet, the hatchet, the pellet, the fret, the indented, the nebulè, and wavy, executed in the best style of Norman work.

Some of the elaborately moulded ribs of the Choir Aisle vaultings are very late Norman.

In the South Aisle (east end) is a Morning Chapel. The stalls here (*temp*. Henry VIII) were brought from the Chancel.

In the South Aisle of Choir a small chantry altar slab was found laid as a gravestone : two of its five crosses can still be traced. It now forms the base of the Communion Table in the Morning Chapel.

A monument to Cornwall (Speaker of the House of Commons, 1789) is in the South Aisle. The mace appears on his monument, because he died whilst actually holding the office of Speaker of the House of Commons ; dying whilst in office entitling a Speaker to that distinctive mark.

The original Pulpit was the work of William Byfleet, Priest of St. Cross, and Rector of Morestead. The present Pulpit was presented to the Church by the late Mr. William Savage, a citizen of Winchester, in memory of a daughter.

———

Canon Humbert, the late Master, gives the following account of the Church as he found it in 1855 :—" It was indeed in what is called 'substantial repair,' and as for cleanliness it seemed to have been periodically limewashed ever since the death of that worthy Master who signalised his reign by completing the whitewashing of the whole Church just three weeks before he expired."

TRIPTYCH IN THE BROTHERS' HALL, ST. CROSS (BY MABUSE).

SOUTH AISLE OF CHURCH.

Inscriptions of Interest, etc.

To John Newles, on a brass near the west entrance of
Church :—

THE YERE OF OUR LORD Mo CCCo Lo AND TWO :
VPON THE XI DAY IN THE MONETH OF FEBEVER :
THE SOUL OF JON NEWLES, THE BODY PASSID FRO :
A BROTHER OF THIS PLACE RESTYNG UNDIR YIS STONE HERE :
BORN IN BEAME [Bearn ?] SQUYER AND SUANT MORE YAN XXX YERE :
UNTO HARRY BEAUFORD BUSSHOP AND CARDINAL :
WHOS SOULES GOD CONVEY AND HIS MODER DERE :
VNTO THE BLISSE OF HEVEN THAT IS ETERNALL. AMEN :

In front of the altar there is a large slab to William
Lewis (a former Master of this Hospital). He was elected
from Hart Hall at Oxford to the Society of Oriel in 1608,
and made provost by the favour of Welshmen. There are
conflicting statements about his character. Cromwell's
party say that his amours were so extraordinary that he was
obliged to fly the country to escape the officers of justice ;
but the Royalists maintain that he was an excellent man,
learned in theology, who went abroad to serve the King.
Anthony Wood, in his *Fasti Oxiensis* says that " he was
made a D. D. by command of the King." He went as
Buckingham's Chaplain—with a sinecure office, I should
think—to the siege of Rochelle.

Canon Humbert states that on the tomb of the Master,
Peter Sancto Mario, in the North Aisle, being accidentally
opened, the features of the venerable occupant, after a lapse
of more than 500 years, were found entire. But in a few
moments all went to dust ; the dress and cape only remaining. These were interwoven with gold and colours,
and for a long time shreds of it were preserved.[1]

[1] *Royal Winchester,* p. 254.

E

In the Morning Chapel are two slabs with quaint inscriptions of the Commonwealth period over the graves of the children of one Laurence :—

SUSANA LAURENCE,
VAS CARNE VALENS.
A FLESH PREVAILING VESSEL FOUND
BEAUTIFIED TO LIE UNDER GROUND.
VIXIT, DEC. 13, 1647.
DEVIXIT, JAN. 18, 1650.

GEORGIUS LAURENTIUS,
EGO UTI LAURUS RIGENS.
I UNDER LY AS LAUREL DRY.
VIXIT, OCT. 14, 1650.
DEVIXIT, SEPT. 29, 1651.

THE FONT.

The Font has a Norman basin on a later base. It was brought from the old church of St. Faith.

St. Cross Church, being in the nature of a conventual chapel, neither had occasion for a font nor was entitled to have the rite of baptism administered within its precincts.[1]

[1] Duthy's *Sketches of Hampshire.*

THE WESTERN DOOR.

Freemasonry and Masons' Marks.

This Church is remarkable for the large number and variety of the masons' marks to be found on its walls. Art in the middle ages was closely involved in the masonic guilds, and these can be traced through the Comacine Guild to the Roman *Collegia*. By the York charter English masonry dates from the time of King Athelstan. Masonry was regarded as a part of geometry, and in the middle ages apprentices were taught the allegory of architecture, while many curious Jewish and Arabian symbols

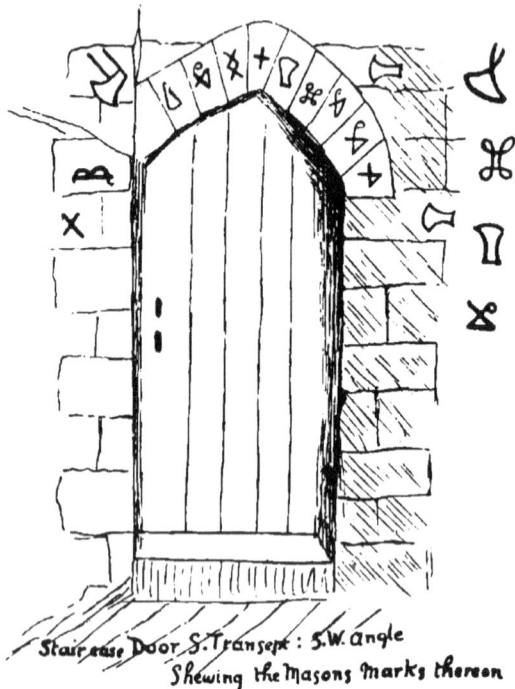

Staircase Door S. Transept : S.W. angle
Shewing the Masons marks thereon

Masons' Marks engrave
Chu

FROM DRAWING

ɩ various Parts of the
of St Cross.

Brother Lewin.

were introduced by the operative masons, who usually
worked under the bishop or abbot as master of the lodge,
and were wont to take the oath of secrecy on the Bible,
the compass, and the square. But the new learning of the
Tudor age superseded the old love of legend and allegory,
and freedom of speech made almost unnecessary the secret
signs and caricatures of the older masons. In the eighteenth
century the tone of freemasonry became lowered, and secret
societies were denounced by Papal authority.

We here reproduce some of the actual marks of the
stone cutters who erected portions of this interesting church
in the twelfth and thirteenth centuries. The voices of these
art workers have long been silent, and the meaning of their
secret signs are alike unknown.

The Burial Ground.

" Divided from the park by a low fence, and to be
recognised by the headstones beyond it, is the quiet little
cemetery ; wherein many of the brothers rest from their
labours, in the blessed hope of a joyful resurrection. It is
a peaceful, bright, and sunny spot ; and is endeared to the
living occupants of the Hospital as the hallowed resting-
place, not only of the long-buried dead of past generations,
but of personal friends whom they have known and loved.
Perhaps nothing presents a truer test of the changed and
improved tone of feeling amongst the brethren, than the
ideas they cherish in regard to this little churchyard." [1]

[1] Canon Humbert's *Memorials of St. Cross.*

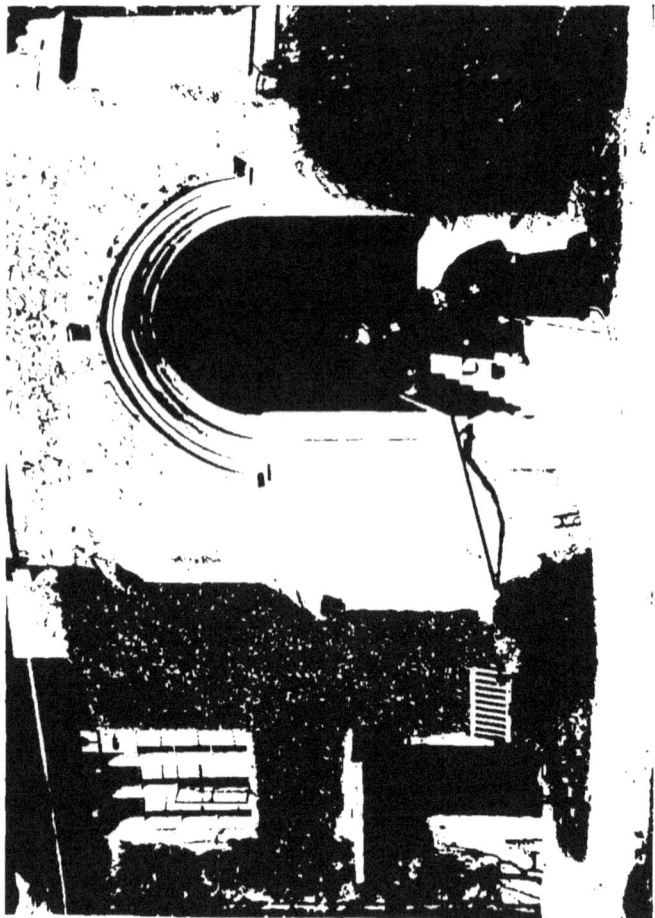

SEVENTEEN RINGS FOR DINNER

This Porch has a fine perpendicular vault with beautifully carved bosses.

VIEW EAST OF THE PORTER'S LODGE.

The Brethren's Hall.

"Built in an age as lavish of architectural beauty on what modern habits would deem a receptacle for beggars as on the noblest of royal palaces."—*Times*.

THE HALL (originally part of the "Hundred Mennes Hall," about thirty-six feet by twenty-four), has four rich fourteenth century windows, and at the east end a dais for the table of officers—those for the Brethren being ranged along the sides. There is yet much to excite interest, and to convey an idea of its original appearance: the ornamental display of Edyndon's roof timbers, the gallery at the end, whence on festivals the cheerful sound of minstrelsy enlivened the banquet; a quaint fifteenth century staircase,[1] and the raised hearth in the centre of the Hall, round which the Brothers are wont to

---

[1] This has Bishop Fox's pelican on the newel vulning its breast.

sit on gaudy-days, and awaken the listlessness of age
by the memories of by-gone days. High up, at the
eastern end, there appears to have been a window
from which the Master could observe from his
chamber in the Tower the behaviour of the Hundred-
Hall poor. The other portion of the Hall has been
adapted as a residence for the Master.

THE BROTHERS' HALL, LOOKING EAST.

In the Master's lodgings specimens of ancient glass may
be seen. Among the subjects are : Christ's presentation in
the Temple : Pontius Pilate washing his hands ; Christ in
the Sepulchre : Cardinal Beaufort's arms.

A piece of 15th century stained glass over the entrance
shows a quartered shield of the arms of France and England,
with a motto--"*a hono et lyesse.*"

THE HALL, ST. CROSS. LOOKING WEST.

The black leathern jacks, the candlesticks, salt cellars, pewter dishes and dinner bell belong to Beaufort's time (1446).

On the east wall is placed an Early German triptych, representing the worship of the Magi, purchased in London by Dr. Lockman, Master of the Hospital (1787–1807).

The porch has a fine Perpendicular vault, with finely carved bosses,

Under the Hall is a groined cellar, of which we give an illustration.

Some of the scenes in *The Warden* and *Henry Dunbar* are represented as occurring in the village of St. Cross.

———

The Ancient Dietary and Doles.

Even during the critical periods in the history of the Hospital, it appears that the Brothers were not neglected :—

In **1350** each of the brethren received daily 5 marks' weight of wheaten bread, 1 "*lagena*" (or *galione*) and-a-half of beer (*mediocris servisie*), a sufficiency of pottage, 3 dishes (*fercula*) at dinner, viz., 1 "*mortrell*" a little mortar or basin of "*wastell*" (the best bread) and milk, 1 dish of meat or fish, and 1 other dish of whatever might be provided for the day (*pitancia juxta exigenciam diei*), and one dish for supper, so that the food and drink (*cibaria et poculenta*) of each brother amounted daily in value to *three pence*. On the vigil of St. Lawrence (which was the Founder's Obit) and the six greater feasts (in addition to 1 dish of better meat or fish) they had 4 "*lagene*" of better beer amongst them ; and each of the Hundred-hall poor, of

This Triptych is considered by some good judges to be the work of Jan de Mabuse, a Flemish painter, famous for the beauty of expression and finish which his portraits possess, and also for the extreme care in the detail of his ornaments, jewels, embroideries, etc. This is to be noticed in the open book, the dagger, the handle of the sword, and the ornaments on the dresses. Jan Mabuse was born in 1492 and died in 1562.

whom 13 were "*pauper iores scolares scole gramaticalis ibidem
missi per magistrum summe scole gramaticalis civitatis
Wynton.*," 1 loaf of barley bread (*panem ordei*), 1 dish of
pulse, 1 salt fish (*allec*), or 2 "*pilchers,*" (or 2 eggs, or
1 farthing's-worth of cheese, Lowth, p. 77), 1 *pocellum* of
beer, or (according to the other account) 3 quarts of small
(*debilis*) beer : to which on the feast days was added 3 loaves
of wheaten bread and some meat.   On Founder's day 200
poor were entertained : 100 received each 1 wheaten loaf,
pottage, a pottle (*pottelum*) of beer, and 1 dish ; and second
hundred half a loaf each.   Besides these there were seven
poor persons, who were choristers, and daily received each
1 wheaten loaf, 1 quart of beer, and 1 dish ; when not
engaged in the church they "*solebant scolas exercere in dicto
hospitali.*" [1]

[1] Woodward's *Hampshire*, p. 234.

THE BREAD ROOM.

The room adjoining this is the ancient Larder.

As to the diet of the Brothers in **1695** (during the mastership of Dr. Lewis) an extract will be of interest, as it describes, with few exceptions, the present rations :—

RARE MENUS!

That there are five Festival days in the year, to wit,— All Saints, Christmas, New Year's-day, Twelfth-day, and Candlemas-day: on which days the brethren have extraordinary commons, and on the eve of which days they have a fire of charcoal in the Common Hall, and one jack of six quarts and one pint of beer extraordinary, to drink together by the fire. And on the said Feast-days they have a fire at dinner, and another at supper in the said hall; and they have a sirloin of beef roasted, weighing forty-six pounds and a half, and three large mince pies,[1] and plum broth, and three joints of mutton for their supper, and six quarts and one pint of beer extraordinary at dinner, and six quarts and one pint of beer after dinner, by the fireside; six quarts and a pint at supper, and the like after supper. And on Wednesdays before Shrove-Tuesdays at dinner every brother hath a pancake; and on Shrove-Tuesdays at dinner every brother hath a pancake besides his commons of beef, and six quarts and one pint of beer extraordinary among them all; and at supper their mutton is roasted, and three hens roasted, and six quarts and a pint of beer extraordinary. And in Lent-time every brother hath in lieu of his commons eight shillings in money paid. And on Palm Sunday the brethren have a green fish, of the

[1] The ingredients of the mince pies and of the plum broth :—two legs of mutton (12lb. weight), 6lb. of beef suet, 3 gallons of fine flour, 3lb. of butter, 3lb. of currants, 3lb. of sun raisins, 2lb of prunes, 1 oz. of nutmeg, 1 oz. of cinnamon, 1 oz. of ginger, 1 oz. of cloves, 1 oz. mace, 1lb. sugar.

value of three shillings and fourpence, and their pot of milk
pottage with three pounds of rice boiled in it, and three
pies with twenty-four herrings baked in them, and six quarts
and one pint of beer extraordinary. And they have on
Good Friday, at dinner, in their pot of beer a cast of bread
sliced, and three pounds of honey, boiled altogether, which
they call honey sop..........And also every brother receives
quarterly eight shillings : viz., six shillings and eightpence
for himself, and sixteenpence to pay his laundress ; and
four shillings paid among them yearly by the tenants of
Yateley. Also, there is allowed by the Master three shillings
and fourpence quarterly to a barber, for the trimming of
the brothers. And upon sealing and renewing of leases
each brother is to have twopence in the pound, for so
many pounds as the fine for renewing the lease amounts
to. And at Christmas, yearly, every brother hath a new
gown made of black cloth rash, of five shillings the yard.

THE CELLAR BENEATH THE BRETHREN'S HALL.

PEWTER DISHES, SKEWERS, ETC., IN THE HOSPITAL KITCHEN.

The Extra Doles.

In modern times the Extra Doles were six in number. They were distributed on All Saints'-eve, Christmas-eve, Easter-eve, Whitsun-eve, the Invention of the Cross, and the Founder's Obit, the 10th of August ; on which occasions the outer gates were closed, and the applicants (sometimes eight hundred in number) admitted one by one at the smaller opening, thence called the dole gate. Each dole consisted of five bushels of flour, producing about four hundred loaves of twelve ounces each. The brethren received each two loaves for themselves, and one for each inmate of their dwellings : the Cook two loaves, the Brewer two loaves, the Barber seven loaves, the Steward and Chaplain six loaves each, the servers of the dole fourteen loaves each : and the remaining, about three hundred loaves, were distributed, one to each of the applicants, at the gate ; any additional applicants receiving one half-penny each in lieu of the dole-bread. On these occasions all sorts of characters were mixed together. There were generally a number of chimney sweeps first, the crowd making way for them. But such gatherings were productive of considerable disorder : and they have been judiciously discontinued for the last ten years ; the money saved being applied to the benefit of the "hundred-hall" poor.[1]

The present Daily Dole.

At present the daily Dole at the Porter's Lodge is two gallons of beer and two loaves of bread, divided into thirty-two portions, supplying a horn of beer and a slice of bread to each wayfarer. The porter states that on the average about thirty wayfarers daily receive this ancient Dole.

[1] Canon Humbert's *Memorials of St. Cross*, pp. 46 and 54.

ENAMELLED SILVER PATEN OF BP. HENRY DE BLOIS' TIME.
[Engraving from Woodward's *Hampshire*.]

The sort of man the Founder was.

"The manner of Carlyle is to reduce all history into biographies, into the action of a few great men upon the world."

BISHOP HENRY DE BLOIS, founder of St. Cross Hospital, was the fourth son of Stephen Count of Blois, half-brother to King Stephen, grandson of William the Conqueror, and Papal Legate. Born in 1101, he was brought up in the monastery of

F

Cluny, and at the age of twenty-eight was made
Bishop of Winchester, which See he ruled forty-two
years. During all this time he retained the Abbacy
of Glastonbury, his tenure of that office extending
over forty-five years. He was a great benefactor
both to Cluny and Glastonbury, and rebuilt many
buildings at the latter place. He was half monk and
half knight ; and was surety to the Archbishop on
Stephen's coronation for his fidelity to the Church.
Later he himself hoped to succeed to the Arch-
bishopric, but as the Pope's refusal was due to the
influence of Stephen and his Queen, he deserted
from the King's party. He pulled down the Conqueror's palace north of Winchester Cathedral, and
strengthened Wolvesey Castle with the materials.
De Blois broke from his allegiance to the Empress,
as she, like Stephen, did not support the Bishop in
his Church policy. Matilda besieged De Blois in
Wolvesey, and De Blois besieged her in Winchester
Castle. The citizens siding with Matilda, De Blois
shot " fiery missiles " from the High tower of Wolvesey Castle, which fired the houses in the lower part of
the City, the fire spreading until most of the houses
and twenty churches were burnt, and also St. Mary's
Abbey, and Hyde Abbey without the walls. The
Empress Matilda made her escape from Winchester
Castle, but the City was sacked. Sixty pounds of
molten silver and fifteen pounds of gold were taken
by De Blois from the ashes of Hyde Abbey ; but in

1167 the Bishop restored the silver cross. De Blois strove to make Winchester a metropolitan see. He was a large collector of art jewellery, statuary, and of beasts and birds. He gave the quaint slatestone font to Winchester Cathedral, and built a treasure house in the South Transept. He made his clergy use silver instead of pewter chalices, and assisted them to obtain them. He built six castles, but during his absence at Cluny Henry II pulled down the tower of Wolvesey, and destroyed the castles of Merdon and Bishop's Waltham. He died in 1173, and lies buried in the plain marble tomb in the centre of the Choir of Winchester Cathedral. His noblest foundation is that of the Hospital of St. Cross. His square set gold ring with a sapphire is still kept in the Library of the Cathedral.

Bp. Henry de Blois lived more than twenty years after founding St. Cross, and no doubt personally superintended the construction and details of the Eastern portion and Transepts of the magnificent Church. The design of Romsey Church is attributed to him, and his work may also be seen in the fine treasury doorways in the South Transept of Winchester Cathedral. After an episcopate of forty-four years his eyes became dim, but his charity remained unstinted, and we are told that he left for himself and his servants barely sufficient maintenance.

The Porter's Lodge.

The portrait of an old Porter, Bro. Bartholomew, who was present at the siege of Gibraltar, may be seen in the Porter's room.

PREPARATIONS FOR THE DAILY DOLE.
(Inside the Porter's Lodge.)

Robert Sherborne, one of the Masters, inserted his favourite motto, " DILEXI SAPIENTIAM," with his initials and date, 1503, in the wall of the Porter's lodge.

SHERBORNE'S MOTTO.—"I HAVE LOVED WISDOM."

An Englishman "goes the rounds."

[Extract from "Royal Winchester."]

SEEING an old gownsman standing about I accosted
him, and asked if he would be so good as to show
me over the hospital.

" Hospital ! " he replied, sharply.   " There ain't no
hospital here.   That's where everybody makes a mistake.
When any of the brethren are ill, we have to send to
Winchester for a doctor."

" Well—the institution," I substituted.

He seemed satisfied with the correction. I found that
there were several persons waiting to be conducted, and
that our guide was a " character."   He was deaf, his speech
was indistinct from the loss of teeth, and he in every
respect came up to the requisite qualification of being
decayed. . . . . .

" Walk this way," said our guide, hobbling on in front
of us.   " Oh ! I won't go too fast for you."

He led us into the church, where we gazed up at
rows of Norman zig-zag until we felt quite giddy. . . . .

" We have heard," said an enquiring lady, who seemed
to take a great interest in everything, " that there is a
beautiful triple arch here. Can we see it ? "

" No, ma'am, you cannot," replied our scrupulous guide ;
" but you will be able to do so when we come to it ! This is
Major Lowth's seat," he added, pointing to one comfortably
cushioned.

"Who is he ?" inquired the lady. " Where does he sit ?"

" Nowhere, ma'am. He does not sit anywhere now.
He is gone to heaven, ma'am—at least, I hope so. He
was one of the trustees." . . . . .

Our guide next directed us to the hall—built in 1440—
and here called attention to the Minstrels' Gallery, etc.

"And who sits in that chair?" asked the inquiring lady,
indicating the principal one at the table.

"Nobody, ma'am," he replied, "at present. But on
gaudy days the Master sits in it."

"Is he one of the brethren?"

"God bless your soul, no, ma'am," he returned; "he's
a minister of the gospel."

We were shown Cardinal Beaufort's rude wooden salt-
cellars and candlesticks, and in the kitchen his battered
round pewter dish, which gave us no great idea of his
splendour; but probably he was doing the humble when
he stayed here.

Thence we went over to the eastern side of the quadrangle, where there is a cloister supporting some decayed
apartments—perhaps erected by De Blois. Here is a table
of Purbeck marble, said to have been used in the Castle,
and which, as it is not round enough for King Arthur, is
usually attributed to King Stephen.

"Would you like to see the nunnery?" inquired our
guide.

We were not aware that there was one, but found that
it consisted of some upper rooms for three nurses. On
asking what there was to see in it, and being told, "Well!
there is a floor," none of us felt very enthusiastic about it.
And so I left this interesting spot—not to return for fifteen
years. Farewell, most conscientious of guides! I am afraid,
alas! that thou art "not sitting anywhere now." I hope
thou too art in heaven![1]

[1] From *Royal Winchester* (p. 248), by REV. A. G. L'ESTRANGE, M.A.

THE CHURCH—FROM THE ITCHEN.

A Castle of Peace patiently Founded in days of trouble.

In this fair spot where Nature is unchecked,
And all the works of God are manifest,
Scarce tainted by the spoiling hand of man,
How many a life has found a blissful close.—ACANTHUS.

THE HOSPITAL OF ST. CROSS, in the suburb of Sparkford, near Winchester, was founded by Bp. Henry de Blois in 1132.

BP. DE BLOIS' TOMB IN THE CHOIR OF WINCHESTER CATHEDRAL.[1]

Bp. Henry de Blois founded St. Cross to support entirely "thirteen poor men, feeble and so reduced in strength that they can hardly or with difficulty support themselves without another's aid "; they were to be provided "with garments and beds suitable to their infirmities, good wheaten bread daily of the weight of 5 marks and three dishes at dinner and one at supper suitable to the day, and drink of good stuff."[2]   Also,

[1] This tomb was formerly said to be that of William Rufus, but his remains are in one of the mortuary chests near the pulpit ; and a paten was found in this tomb, which is a thing not likely to be put in the coffin of William Rufus.

[2] Any Brother, if he should recover his strength, "to be sent abroad with honour and reverence, and another put in his place."

a hundred other poor and indigent men were to have their dinner daily, and other acts of kindness done to the poor according to the ability of the Hospital. To this object he appropriated the tithes of twelve parishes in the diocese, two in that of Salisbury, and one in that of Lincoln, with other rents in Winchester; and in 1151 handed over his new foundation to the charge of Raymund, master of the Knights Hospitallers of Jerusalem. The next Bishop of Winchester, Richard Toclyve, added to the charity the benefaction of feeding another hundred poor men daily. This extension of the original purpose of the Foundation rendered it it necessary—or, at least, useful—to maintain a new staff of officers, and four priests, thirteen secular clerks, and several choristers were introduced, and payment partly in beer and meat given to them.[1]

Interesting Ceremony at the Induction of a Master in 1204.

TO all the faithful in Christ, Peter de Rupibus, by the grace of God, Bishop of Winchester, eternal greeting in the Lord. Among the works of piety it is not esteemed the least when the benefit of the poor is respected, and their support so provided for that it may with prudent discernment continue and remain; the Scripture bearing witness, which declares, "Blessed is the man who considereth the poor and needy, the Lord shall

---

[1] From a Paper by Rev. Canon Humbert.

deliver him in the time of trouble." Wherefore we, desirous
to take heed that the distribution of alms to be made to
the Poor of Christ by the constitution of the Lord Henry
the Bishop, in the House of St. Cross, Winchester, may not
be defrauded or perish, have elected Mr. Alan de Stoke,
whom we know to be a prudent and faithful man, and
have committed to him the cure of the said House with
the appurtenances, to have and to hold freely, and quietly,
and peaceably for the whole time of his life, saving to us
and to our successors our authority and dignity therein.
And, in testimony of this appointment, we have made to
him the present charter confirmed with our seal.

A Master inducted in A.D. 1345.

The ceremony was as follows :—

"On the 14th day of May, A.D., 1345, after the hour of
vespers, before the gate of the Hospital or House of
St. Cross, near Winchester, in the presence of the notary
public, and other witnesses, the venerable man Mr. Raymund
Pelegrini, Canon of London, presented and exhibited
certain letters apostolical ; to wit, one of grace, and another
executory, of our lord the Pope, being true leaden bulls,
sealed after the manner of the Roman Court, not vitiated
nor cancelled, but free from all error and suspicion,—to the
venerable man Mr. John de London, rector of the church
of Esher in the diocese of Winchester, the sub-executor
concerning the provision or grace in such process, together
with other his colleagues." The Deed goes on to describe
" the said letters apostolical ; to wit, the one of grace with

silken threads, and the other executory with canvas threads;"
...and proceeds :—" Forthwith the said Mr. John, by the
delivery of the principal door of the said Hospital, and
afterwards of the bell-ropes, delivered into the hands of the
said Mr. Raymund, did, by the apostolic authority
committed to him, actually and effectually induct the said
Mr. Raymund Pelegrini into the corporal possession of the
same Hospital or House, and all its rights and appurtenances;
and subsequently, the same Mr. John advancing to the high
altar of the church, in fuller token of such possession,
delivered and assigned to the said Mr. Raymund a book, to
wit, a missal ; and a chalice :......the rector of the church
of Alresford, and others in very great numbers, the servants
and ministers of the Hospital, being present."

The quaint pomp "gone for ever."

In respect to this interesting ceremony Canon
Humbert remarks :—

How much one would like, by some magic charm, to
recall that spectacle of more than five hundred years ago !
The church itself looking much as it now does ; its western
pinnacles just completed, the nave-roof recently leaded,
the fine west window in all its beauty. But how different
all else ! Beaufort's tower and refectory not built ;—
De Campeden's work not thought of ;—the brethren's
houses probably at the south and east sides of the church,
where the marks of the original cloister, and the blocked
up entrance to the south transept, still remain ; and where
the foundations of the old buildings may be traced. But

let us look a little further. The external ceremony is over : the papal letters have been duly inspected, and are clearly " true leaden bulls, duly sealed, and free from error ;" the silken and canvas threads are all right ; the great western door is formally delivered. And now, the procession enters the church ; and, after the bell has been tolled under the tower, how much we should like to follow Master John and Master Raymund in their advance to the high altar ; and see the furniture and decorations and plate; and compare notes with the present aspect of things. But the vespers at St. Cross, and the quaint pomp and circumstance of five hundred years ago, are gone by for ever ; and, however they may excite our imagination, can never be reproduced.[1]

[1] Canon Humbert's *Memorials of St. Cross*, p. 22.

CARDINAL BEAUFORT'S CHAIR.

Master William de Edyngdon.

This Master (1346), afterwards bishop of Winchester, according to an ancient document, found the church unfinished and thatched with straw. He roofed the nave with lead, inserted and glazed the clerestory windows, built the pinnacles at the west end, and erected a chamber for the Master.

What the Hospital of St. Cross was in 1350.

Similar Institutions bear the name Domus Dei, Maison Dieu (Dover), God's House (Southampton), God's Love House (Beverley).

In the year 1350 the establishment consisted of the Master, who got £8 a year ; four priests at 13s. 4d. a year ; thirteen secular clerks who were boarded, lodged, and clothed ; a varying number of choristers from two to seven, who in the intervals of singing "went to school," and lived on the leavings of the Master and Brethren !

THE STAIRCASE IN HALL.

The "Hundred Hall Poor," the poorest in the city, of good character, were provided every day with a loaf of bread, three quarts of beer, and two messes for their dinner, in the *Hundred Mennes-Hall* ; and they were permitted to carry home with them whatever they did not consume ; and thirteen of the poorer scholars of the great grammar school of Winchester were daily included in the number.

The precise period when the daily entertainment to the one hundred poor, as directed by the Founder, ceased is not known, as the practice is not even mentioned in the Custumary by which the Hospital is now governed, and therefore had been discontinued for many years previous to the drawing up of the Custumary in 1696.[1]

[1] Moody's *History of St. Cross Hospital*, p. 13.

The hospital survives stormy times.

Throughout its stormy history, the essential features of the Hospital, the thirteen poor men and the Church, have remained on their present site. After Henry de Blois' death, a long struggle took place between the Hospitallers and the succeeding Bishops, and it was not till the reign of Edward I that the knights finally gave up the contest.

Spoilers of the Hospital.

IN 1372 the Hospital had to be rescued from the spoiler. William of Wykeham, as Bishop of Winchester, had to take proceedings, which oocupied over seventeen years, against the Master, a certain Roger de Cloune, who claimed the Hospital as his own ecclesiastical sinecure benefice, and refused to render accounts. The evidence taken gives a life-like picture of a medieval Hospital :—

The Master had set himself to despoil the Hospital during the remaining time of his incumbency. "He sold the corn and the cattle, and a great quantity of materials that had been laid in for repairs, and converted the money to his own use : while the suit was pending he had the impudence to pull down the larder of the Hospital, and to sell the materials. Indeed, it was now of no use ; the great hall was fallen in ; the hundred poor were turned away ; and the thirteen brethren were forced to quit the Hospital and provide for themselves where they could." Wykeham saw that a further effort was required, and declared that "the whole revenue ought to be applied to the use of

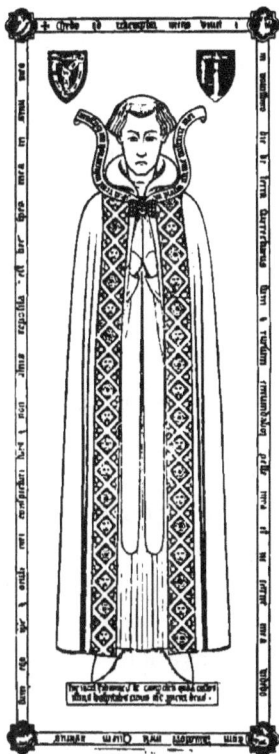

JOHN DE CAMPEDEN, WARDEN

CHURCH OF THE HOSPITAL OF ST CROSS WINCHESTER

the poor," and this principal was affirmed by a Commission, dated 23rd February, 1372, as well as by a bull of Gregory XI, 25th February, in the same year.[1]

A Worthy Master.

Better times followed during the Mastership of John de Campeden, Wykeham's friend and executor, which extended from the year 1382 to 1410, and he is recorded as having spent on new buildings and repairs the then enormous sum of £1,822 (=£27,000 of our money).

Amongst other things, he built, in 1390, eleven chambers for the thirteen brethren. These buildings are said to have stood on the south of the Church.

John de Campeden survived his great patron five years. He lies buried in the church. His memorial brass, on which are his armorial bearings, the emblems of our Lord's Passion, is within the communion rails ; it is in excellent preservation. (*See illustration.*)

The words chosen by him for his monumental inscription are—

Credo q⁰· redemptor meus vivit et in novifsimo die surrecturus fum de terra et rurfum circumdabor pelle mea et in carne videbodeum falvatorᵐ· meum quem vifurus fum ego ipse et oculi mei con fpecturi funt et non alius repofita eft ßec fpes mea in finu meo.

TRANSLATION.

I know that my Redeemer liveth, etc.—*Job* xix, 25-27.

Round the neck :—

Jesu, when Thou comest in judgment, condemn me not ;
Thou Who fashionedst me, have mercy on me.

---

[1] *Wykeham's Register*, vol. ii, edited by T. F. Kirby, p. 28, *seq.*

UNDER ST. CATHERINE'S HILL.

Cardinal Beaufort.

" The men of each age must be judged by the ideal of their own age and country."

CARDINAL BEAUFORT, born in 1377, was a son of John of Gaunt, half-brother of Henry IV, and tutor to both Henry V and Henry VI. He was four times Lord Chancellor of England, and fills a great space in the Lancastrian times, combining the positions of bishop, statesman, almost soldier, and banker to the royal family, for he lent £22,000 at one time to Henry V, and the regal crown itself was pawned to him. He gave a sum equal to half-a-million to raise 250 lances and 4000 archers to put down the Hussites in Bohemia, but he diverted this army to aid his country in the war in France. Perhaps the most romantic incident connected with his great career is his reported presence at the burning of Joan of Arc at Rouen : the Cardinal is said to have burst into tears, and to have left the horrible scene. The unhappy part which he took in the trials of Sir John Oldcastle for heresy, and the Duchess of Gloucester for witchcraft and treason ; his persecution of the Lollards ; his death as pictured erroneously by Shakspere ; his gift of £1000 towards the rebuilding of London Bridge ; his beautiful Cross which he erected in Winchester High Street ; his munificence to the London prisoners and prisons ; and his enlargement, repair, and endowment of St. Cross Hospital—make his Chantry in Winchester

G

Cathedral worthy of contemplation both for the occupant and its own splendour.[1]   He died at Wolvesey
Castle April 11th, 1447.   Part of the inscription round
his tomb was :—

"I SHOULD BE IN ANGUISH DID I NOT KNOW THY MERCIES."

BROTHERS OF CARDINAL BEAUFORT'S FOUNDATION.

"The Almshouse of Noble Poverty."

Cardinal Beaufort, Wykeham's successor, towards
the end of his life, designed a new foundation of St.
Cross, to be called "The Almshouse of Noble Poverty."
The first Foundation was for the poorest of the poor ;

[1] *Lecture on Cardinal Beaufort and his Times*, by Rev. Dr. Fearon.

this was to be for what used to be called the second
poor—people like Dogberry and Verges, who had
once " had everything handsome about them," but
had " had losses." There were to be two priests,
thirty-five brethren, and three sisters, and the brethren
were to be " noblemen or members of our family,"
i.e., men of gentle birth or people who have been
employed in the Cardinal's own service. The endowments he purported to give would have made the
foundation one of the richest in the country. It
was, however, never completed. A large part of the
intended revenues was to be derived from manors
granted in reversion, which manors, it seems, never
came into possession. The Wars of the Roses super-
vened. What property had come in was mostly
lost, and in 1486 Waynflete reduced the permanent
forces of the new foundation to one chaplain and
two brethren.[1]

The hospital after the Reformation.

ON the 20th September, A.D. 1535, a Visitation of
the Hospital was made by Dr. Thomas Leigh,
Commissary of the famous and honourable man, Master
Thomas Cromwell, Visitor-General of the most illustrious
Prince in Christ, Henry VIII. Such a visitation was no
light matter to the religious houses of that day ; and, for
the most part, was the precursor of their dissolution. But
St. Cross endured the scrutiny of the Visitor-General ; who

[1] From *The Times*, April 11th, 1896.

only found "certain things requiring reformation." After
referring to the qualifications and support of the thirteen
Brothers, he orders that the poor men shall have sufficient
and proper clothing and food within the said House, according to the will of the Founder, and that it *be not given them
in money* counted in any manner for the same. Also that
the hundred-hall-poor shall not be served at the gates as
mendicants, like as was not long ago accustomed to be done;
and such dinners shall be distributed to them who study and
labour with all their strength at handywork to obtain food :
and, in no case, shall such alms be afforded to strong, robust,
and indolent mendicants, like so many that wander about
such places, who ought rather to be driven away with staves,
as drones and useless burdens upon the earth. And also,
some discreet and honest priest of the House shall hear
and teach the poor inhabitants here the Lord's prayer, and
the Apostles' creed *in English* ; which prayer and creed
all the poor men shall say together in the Church before
dinner. And also the Master, or President, shall not
exhibit reliques, images, or miracles, when sought for ; but
shall earnestly exhort pilgrims and guests to give to the
poor and needy what they would have offered for such
purposes. And also the Master shall in nowise diminish
the number of the priests, presbyters, sacrists, and others
within this House, that have been used to minister here, on
the Foundation, or by custom ; and he shall observe all
and singular other things unbroken which the Foundation
aforesaid, or laudable custom, have hitherto required to be
done here. Also, he shall have in this House a library,
in which, besides other necessary books, shall be placed
printed volumes of the New and Old Testaments, the works

ORIEL TO NUNNES ROOM OVER AMBULATORY.

of Jerome, Augustine, Theophylact, and others of the most ancient fathers of a similar kind.

————

More Spoilers.

IN 1557 the Master, Dr. Robert Raynolds, contrived to lease away part of the Hospital property, not only of a great part of the Mansion House of the said Hospital, with the bakehouse and brewhouse, orchards, gardens, and closes adjoining, and heretofore kept in the proper occupation and use of the Hospital for the better housekeeping and sustentation of the poor ; but also, of certain rents of wheat and malt, and also of one little manor called Ashton, of the yearly value of ten pounds. After divers great and trouble- some suits in law, to the great travail and expense of John Watson, clerk, now Master of the said Hospital, it was enacted by authority of Parliament, that both the said leases be made void, and of none effect against the now Master and Brethren ; and to avoid the like in time to come provi- sion was made to prevent the leasing out in future of the premises and lands within the precincts of the Hospital of St. Cross and parish of St. Faith.[1]

In 1538 the Master was commanded to deliver to the Vicar-General, the charters of the first, second, and third foundations, together with the charters of donations and the appropriation of churches; and also the bulls, privileges, and other popish muniments belonging to the house ; to- gether with a true and faithful inventory of its moveable effects, as well as a rental of its fixed and landed property.[2]

[1] Canon Humbert's *Memorials of St. Cross*, p. 39.
[2] Moody's *History of St. Cross Hospital*, p. 12.

In 1632, the Master, Dr. Lewis, in answer to an inquiry made by Archbishop Laud, reported, that he had granted no lease or received any fine, but that the three last Masters had converted all the leases, save one of the value of £40 per annum, into a term of three lives; and that the fines received by his predecessors had not been expended upon the Hospital buildings, which he found in extreme ruin and dilapidation.

In 1696 some of the earlier Brethren's houses were pulled down, and a Master's residence was formed out of a portion of the quadrangle.

In 1789 the south side of quadrangle was razed to the ground.

The system of receiving fines on granting leases was continued by several of the Masters of the Hospital. It left but a small income to the Hospital, and the abuse was brought to light in 1853.

OUTSIDE OF CHANCEL AND NORTH TRANSEPT.

BROTHERS READING THE LOCAL NEWSPAPER.

Che Master's Chambers, etc.

Before the Reformation the Master's Chambers were partly in Beaufort's Tower and over the present Porter's Lodge. Subsequently some of the Brothers' houses and part of the Hundred Mennes Hall were made into a dwelling for the Master. Recently a new house for the Master has been erected north of Beaufort's Tower, outside the gates ; and it is proposed to make the Master's old quarters into ten more sets of rooms for the Brethren, making in all accommodation for twenty-seven brothers.

The silver cross worn by the Brothers is at the death of one of them placed on a red velvet cushion and laid on his breast in the coffin ; and then before burial it is taken off, and the Master fastens it on the gown of the next Brother.

The gowns worn at the present time by the Brethren of both Foundations are similar both in colour and make to those worn by them in the reign of Henry VI.

It may be as well to add that the advantages of the two Brotherhoods are free to the whole of England.

THE SILVER SEAL OF THE HOSPITAL.

The Arms of the Hospital is at the foot of the Cross. The legend around it may be translated—"The Seal of the Corporate House of the Holy Cross, near Winchester."

The hospital Deeds and Registers.

The Reformation in no way interfered with the Hospital; but in 1666 some of the charters and registers are said to have been burnt by the widow of the then Steward (one Mr. Wright), to hide her husband's defalcations. The oldest register in possession of the Master dates from September 25th, 1676.

The New Scheme.

"The links seem unbroken between the past and the present."

UNDER the new scheme the two Foundations are treated as separate Institutions under one head, and the difference in the qualifications of the two classes of Brethren are carefully laid down. After 250 years of effacement the Brethren of Beaufort's Almshouse again are recognised by the distinctive gown and badge, namely, a red gown with a Cardinal's hat and tassels embroidered on the left breast of the gowns. A portion of the income is dedicated to the maintenance of fifty out-pensioners, as representing the original outlay upon the Hundred Hall poor under the trusts of the Hospital of St. Cross. Thus the original purpose of each Foundation has been once again most carefully maintained.

The Present Trustees.

THE MASTER OF ST. CROSS.

(Rev. G. W. Andrewes, M.A.)

A List of the Masters of St. Cross.

——	ROBERT DE LIMESIA	This name occurs in a copy of the Founder's charter.
1185	ROGER ————	… Appointed by Bp. Toclyve.
1208	ALAN DE STOKE	
· — —	HUMFREY DE MYLERS	
1241	HENRY DE SECUSIA	Presented by King Hen. III.
——	GALFRID DE FERINGES	
1260	THOMAS DE COLCHESTER	
——	STEPHEN DE WOTTON	
1289	PETER DE SANCTO MARIO	Archdeacon of Surrey.
1296	WILLIAM DE WENLYNGE	
1299	ROBERT DE MAYDENESTAN	Deprived 1305. Restored; still Master, 1313.
1321	GALFRID DE WELLEFORD	Presented by the King.
1322	BERTRAND DE ASSERIO	
1332	PETER DE GALICIANO	
1334	WILLIAM DE EDYNDON	Afterwards Bishop of Winchester.
1345	RAYMUND PELEGRINI	
1346	RICHARD DE LUTESHALL	
1346	JOHN DE EDYNDON	
1366	WILLIAM DE STOWELL	
1367	RICHARD DE LYNTESFORD	
1370	ROGER DE CLOUNE	Deprived 1374.
1374	NICHOLAS DE WYKEHAM	
1382	JOHN DE CAMPEDEN	Archdeacon of Surrey. Buried at St. Cross.
1410	JOHN FORREST	Afterwards Archdeacon of Surrey and Dean of Wells.
1444	THOMAS FORREST	Died at St. Cross.
1463	THOMAS CHAUNDELER, D.D.	Resigned 1465. Warden of New College.
1465	WILLIAM WESTBURY, S.T.B.	Provost of Eton College.
1473	RICHARD HARWARD, LL.D.	… Buried at St. Cross.
1489	JOHN LYCHEFIELD	
1492	ROBERT SHERBORNE	… Afterwards Bishop of St. David's, and of Chichester.
1508	JOHN CLAYMUND	
1524	JOHN INCENT, LL.D.	… Also Dean of St. Paul's.

1545	WILLIAM MEADOWE, M.A. ...	Prebendary of Winchester.
1557	JOHN LEEFE, D.D.	Buried in Chapel of Winchester College.
1557	ROBERT REYNOLLS, D.D. ...	Ejected on accession of Elizabeth.
1559	JOHN WATSON, M.D. ...	Afterwards Bishop of Winchester, and held the Mastership by Royal Dispensation till 1583.
1583	ROBERT BENETT, S.T.P. ...	Afterwards Bishop of Hereford.
1603	ARTHUR LAKE, D.D. ...	Afterwards Bishop of Bath and Wells.
1616	SIR PETER YOUNG, Knight	
1628	WILLIAM LEWIS, S.T.P.	Deposed by Cromwell. Restored 1660. Buried at St. Cross.
1648	JOHN LISLE (M.P. for Winchester)	Made a Peer by Cromwell, and President of the High Court of Justice.[1]
1657	JOHN COOKE ...	Solicitor to Parliament ; beheaded at the Restoration.
1669	HENRY COMPTON, D.D. ...	Afterwards Bishop of Oxford and of London.
1676	WILLIAM HARRISON, D.D.	Prebendary of Winchester.
1694	ABRAHAM MARKLAND, D.D.	Prebendary of Winchester. Buried at St. Cross.
1728	JOHN LYNCH, D.D.	Afterwards Dean of Canterbury.
1760	JOHN HOADLY, LL.D. ...	Chancellor of the Diocese, etc.
1776	BEILBY PORTEUS, D.D. ...	Afterwards Bishop of Chester and of London.
1788	JOHN LOCKMAN, D.D. ...	Canon of Windsor.
1807	FRANCIS NORTH, M.A., Earl of Guildford	
1855	LEWIS MACNAUGHTAN HUMBERT, M.A.	Resigned, 1868.
1868	W. G. ANDREWES, M.A. ...	The present Master.

[1] His widow was beheaded in Winchester Market Square in 1685 by order of Judge Jeffreys.

The Income of the Hospital at various times.

A.D.						£	s	d
1370.—The income at this date was ...						300	0	0 [1]

[As reckoned by Bishop William of Wykeham.]

1526.—The income at this date was ...						496	18	$4\frac{1}{2}$ [1]
1534-5.	„	„	„	„	„ ...	281	13	5 [1]
1621.	„	„	„	„	„ ...	200	0	0 [2]
1835-6.	„	„	„	„	„ ...	1112	7	5 [1]
1857.	„	„	„	„	„ ...	1722	2	4 [3]
1898.	„	„	„	„	about	4000	0	0

1912.   It has been computed that by this date the income will probably be increased to   ...   ... } 8652 17 11 [4]

1818-38.   During this period the Master received over £53,000 in fines on renewing leases ; and the average annual income of the Master appeared to be little less than £1,400.[1]

Salaries, Stipends, and Allowances in A.D. 1526.[5]

	£	s	d
To fifteen persons, described as Chaplains and Clerks, —stipends, £35. 4s.; allowances, £5. 16s. 4d. ...	£41	0	4
To Choristers	5	17	$6\frac{1}{4}$
To eleven poor Brethren,—stipends, £7. 3s. 4d.; allowances, £3. 6s. 8d.	10	10	0
Extra allowances to three Brethren	1	12	6
Allowances, at 10d. per week, to the whole of the Brethren	21	19	2
Wages to servants, barber, and washing	8	5	10
Alms to poor in Hundred Men's Hall	6	18	8
Doles at six feasts, 5s. each; wheat on ditto, 5s. each; alms on Sundays and Holy days, £3. 5s.; peas for Hundred Men's Hall	6	9	8
	£102	13	$8\frac{1}{2}$

---

[1] Woodward's *Hampshire*, p. 239.   [2] Inquiry by Archbishop Laud.
[3] Humbert's *Memorials of St. Cross*, p. 83.
[4] As valued by Mr. Tite, M.P.
[5] Moody's *History of St. Cross Hospital*, p. 12.

THE LATE MASTER OF ST CROSS (REV. CANON L. M. HUMBERT, M.A.)
who superintended the Restorations.

Events of Interest connected with St. Cross.

1136.   Founded by Bishop Henry de Blois.
1137.   Management given to the Knights of St. John of Jerusalem.
1151.   The eastern portion and transepts of church built.
1185.   Hospitallers surrendered Hospital to Bp. Toclive.
1187.   Hospital given back to Hospitallers by the Pope.
1189.   Granted to Hospitallers by Richard I.
1197.   Awarded to Bp. of Winchester by Pope's arbitration.
1199.   Given back to Hospitallers by King John.
1200.   Finally assigned to Bp. of Winchester.
1255.   The west end of church not finished at this date. Bp. Ethelmar invited assistance for its completion.
1321.   Inquiry into defects of the Hospital by Bp. Reginald de Asserio.
1336.   Hospital buildings repaired and nave roof leaded ; Hundred-mennes hall roofed and chambers built for the Master.
1372.   Lengthy inquiry instituted by Bishop William of Wykeham.
1379.   Muniments and records handed over by Hospitallers to Bp. William of Wykeham.
1382.   Appointment of John de Campeden as Master, who expended equal to £27,000 on repairs, etc.
1384.   Tower of Church rebuilt and Aisles roofed ; the encaustic tiles laid.
1385.   High Altar of alabaster erected.
1446.   Almshouse of Noble Poverty founded in conjunction with the Hospital by Cardinal Beaufort, for thirty-five additional Brothers and three Hospital Nurses.
1461.   The estates comprising the Beaufort Endowments were reclaimed by the Crown on the accession of the House of York.

BISHOP WILLIAM OF WYKEHAM.

This great and vigilant Bishop rescued the Hospital from the spoiler. The proceedings occupied seventeen years, and were carried on at great cost to the Bishop.

The above portrait is taken from the original painting in the Hall of Winchester College.

1486. Owing to lack of funds, Bp. Waynflete reduces Beaufort's Foundation to one Priest and two Brethren.

1509. Parish Church of St. Faith pulled down. The Font and bell were removed to the Hospital Church.

1527. A reward of twelvepence given to the parishioners of Twyford, coming with banners at the Feast of Whitsuntide.

1509-47. Carved Stalls, now in Morning Chapel, erected.

1535. The Hospital, and its choral services, survived the Reformation. The Vicar General reported that "certain things" required reformation ; and sturdy beggars were to be repulsed.

1616. The ancient Register of the Hospital burnt by the widow of the then Steward.

1632. A stringent inquiry made by Archbishop Laud. The Master, Dr. Lewis, reported that he found the Hospital in extreme ruin and dilapidation.

1648-55. During the Commonwealth, the regicides Lisle and Cooke acted as Master.

1694. "Custumary" for the management of the Hospital drawn up by Dr. Markland.

1737. The clock erected in the Church Tower by William Skikelthorp, of London.

1744. Owing to dampness of Church, daily evensong discontinued.

1763. Licence to the Master by Bishop Hoadley to pull down and destroy the Ambulatory, etc., on the eastern side of quadrangle, and to convert the materials to the use of the Hospital. Happily this was never acted on.

1789. Beaufort's houses on the south of quadrangle pulled down.

1848-53. Chancery suits resulting in a new scheme.

[The law-suits to obtain these orders cost £5,600.]

VIEW FROM THE HOME PARK.

The Home Park and Meadows.

These are situated on the south of the Hospital, and are well wooded, the "fishful Itchen," so loved by Izaak Walton, that prince of fishermen, flowing on its way to Southampton Water by the side of the foot-path which leads to Twyford. When the hay is cut, the mowers claim a "jack" of beer, and when a tree is blown or cut down the aged brethren may be seen actively carrying home their share of "lop and top."

Our illustration shows St. Catherine's Hill in the background. This hill has a miz-maze on the top. The deep vallum, extending over a thousand yards in circuit, is an old British earthwork, which would take 3,300 men for its defence.[1]

[1] Shore's *Hampshire*, p. 23.

A BIT OF OLD GLASS (ST. GREGORY)
IN THE NORTH-WEST CLERESTORY WINDOW.

The Staff of the Hospital.

In 1350.

The Master.
13 Brethren.
The Steward.
13 "Clerici."
7 Choristers.
4 "Capellani."
2 Servants (garsiones).
3 Bakers.
3 Brewers.
1 Cook.
1 "Curtilarius."
2 "Lotrices."
3 "Caractarii."
8 Horses and 3 carts.

In 1486

Beaufort's Foundation, in addition to the regular Foundation, consisted of:

1 Priest.
2 Brethren.

In 1632.

The Master.
13 Brethren.
The Chaplain.
The Steward.
12 Out-Brethren.
28 Out-Sisters.
2 Probationers.

In 1899.

The Master.
Curate.
13 Brethren.
4 Beaufort's Men.
The Steward.
The Receiver.
50 Male and Female Out-Pensioners.

The Founder's Tomb in Winchester Cathedral.

[Sometimes called Rufus' Tomb.]

Bishop Henry de Blois, the first Founder of St. Cross Hospital died in 1171, and was buried before the high altar in Winchester Cathedral. During his Episcopate De Blois "chested" the remains of Canute, Rufus, and other princes and prelates, and two of these original chests are still inside the two most easterly mortuary chests which Bp. Fox placed on the choir screens in 1525. St. Ethelwold was buried in the south crypt, Bp. Walkelyn, the Norman builder, sleeps amid his work in the nave, and St. Swithun's bones were enshrined behind the high altar.

In 1683 this tomb was accepted without question as the tomb of Rufus, but it was then believed to be empty ; and when before this, in 1642, it was broken open by the rebels, a small silver chalice was found therein, shewing conclusively that the remains were those of some notable ecclesiastic. Whose tomb could this be if it were not that of Bp. Henry de Blois, who is expressly stated to have been buried before the High Altar? If this tomb had been that of Rufus, and if it had stood under the great tower, it would probably have been broken or damaged when the tower fell. Stowe, writing in 1592, records that the bones of Rufus had been translated and laid in a coffin with Canute's bones, long before that time, while in this tomb are still to be found the remains of its occupant.

When it was opened, August 28th, 1868, in the presence of four medical men and the cathedral architect, the interior cavity was found to measure 6ft. 8in. with a depth

of about 21in. to 22in. In the bottom were certain holes,
probably for the exudation of moisture. The remains found
were those belonging to one skeleton of a male measuring
5ft. 8in. to 5ft. 10in. It is not quite complete in all its
parts ; many of the bones were much decayed and broken,
but nine of the teeth were remarkably sound and good.
There were also found:—a piece of ivory carving representing a lion's head [1] (symbolical of the Redeemer, the lion of
the tribe of Judah), possibly the curved end of a pastoral
staff, the iron ferule with portions of the wooden shaft
tapering from 1½in. to 1in. in diameter remaining[2]; a
small oval turquoise parted from the setting ; various
fragments of red-brown cloth, striped muslin, closely woven
muslin, coarser muslin, twill serge-like material with fine
threads, thick coarse fibre twill, linen with threads running
across at regular intervals, thick firm cloth, ribbed braid,
seven different patterns of gold braid, minute particles of
lead with the dust, half a dozen iron nails, small pieces of
twig with bark on, some pieces of cork, and a few nutshells,
these latter being accounted for by the presence of mice,
indicated by a small burrow found beneath the tomb.

The base or hollowed stone coffin consists of an oolitic
block, measuring 7ft. 5in. in length, by 3ft. 2½in. at the head
and 2ft. 4½in. at foot, the height of this lower block being
1ft. 5in. above the pavement. As a lid to this lower stone
coffin there rests a massive coped Purbeck slab (*dos d'âne*[3]),
polished, its thickness at the top of the ridge being 11in.
This upper slab has been wrought to its present shape with

---

[1] Similar to knocker, Sanctuary Door, Durham.
[2] See Pastoral Staff on Seal of Bp. Langton, British Museum.
[3] Ass's back.

much labour. At the bottom of the lower stone a chamfer has been worked all around.

The tomb bears no inscription, cross, or ornament, save only a flat fillet in relief bordering all the edges of the coping.

Milner hazards the opinion that De Blois enshrined some of the bones of his uncle, Rufus, leaving the rest in this tomb; but as the almost perfect skeleton of its occupant remains to this day, the reference to De Blois' times seems to strengthen the evidence that this is none other than the tomb of the famous Bishop Henry De Blois. This opinion is held by Dr. Kitchin (Dean of Durham) and by many learned antiquarians.

For much of the information given above we are indebted to an exhaustive Paper communicated in 1870 to the Society of Antiquaries by Rev. J. G. Joyce, F.S.A.,[1] to which the reader is referred.

---

[1] *The Archæologia*, Vol. xlii, pp. 309-321.

Portrait of Brother Bartholomew.

(See page 9.)

This Brother was a native of Sherborne, Dorsetshire, and had been a soldier in Queen Anne's reign. He was present at the taking of Gibraltar in 1704, and was many years Porter at this Hospital. He died aged ninety and upwards. An oil painting of Brother Bartholomew is to be seen at the Porter's Lodge, at the back of which his age is given as 102.

APPENDIX.

Extracts from the Report of the Charity Commissioners, 1836.

I.

Customary of 1696.

The custom there was, and had been time out of memory, that the Hundred Hall should consist of forty poor men and women, namely, twelve poor men and twenty-eight poor women, and two reversioners, who were to receive from the Steward every Sunday, 1*d.* each, and were to have, namely, four sheep's hinges, and soup made for them of the hinges every Sunday, Tuesday, and Thursday, to be divided among them in the room called the Hundred Hall; and also on those days a peck of wheat of the house-made bread, made and baked into forty little loaves; that they were to have a barrel of beer every time they brewed for the house, and that the twenty-eight women were to have on Fridays for dinner, milk pottage and three and a half casts of wheat bread, and one pint of beer each, and in Lent a peck of peas boiled in lieu of the sheep's hinges, at dinner, and 9*d.* each in lieu of the herrings formerly allowed them in Lent. That it was the custom that there should be three bushels of malt toll free for every hogshead of beer; and that the Porter was to receive every day from the Butler a cast of bread and three quarts of beer, to relieve at the gate such poor persons as came and craved relief there.

VAULTING OF THE PORCH TO BROTHERS' HALL.

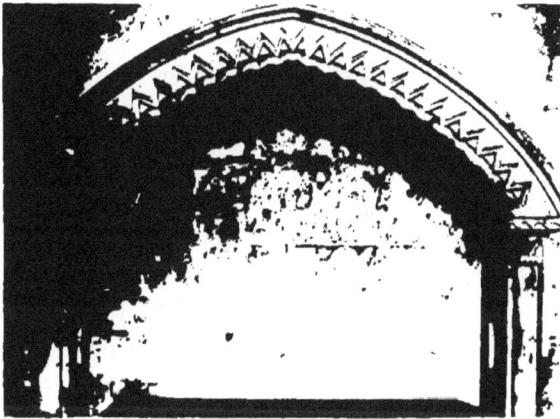

REMAINS OF ALTAR TO ST. THOMAS OF CANTERBURY, SOUTH TRANSEPT,
WITH TRACES OF PAINTING ON BACK WALL.

That it was the custom that there should be six doles
in the year, namely, Christmas Eve, Easter Eve, the 3rd
of May (finding of the Holy Cross), Whitsun Eve, the
10th of August (the Founder's obit), and the Eve of All
Saints, on which days there were to be distributed among
such as should come for them, in little loaves, eight bushels
of wheaten bread, amounting to between 700 and 800, and
if the number of poor people should be more than the
number of loaves should suffice, then the Steward was to
give to every other person one half-penny in lieu thereof.
All which customs and usages the said Master, Brethren,
Steward, and Chaplain did respectfully and jointly promise
to observe and keep.

II.

In the choice of the Brethren, there is no restriction
as to age, place of birth, or residence, but they have been
usually selected from decayed tradesmen who have attained,
or are verging towards, sixty years of age. In two or
three instances, domestic servants from the household of
the Master or his connexions have been admitted. The
Hundred Hall poor are forty in number, and are persons
of all ages of either sex, but are usually resident in
Winchester or its immediate neighbourhood.

The income of the Hospital arises from two sources,
namely, from the pensions or payments from the Churches
mentioned in the grant of Henry de Blois, reserved rents
on tithes and lands let on lease for years or lives, the tithes
of St. Faith, corn rents reserved on the leases of the
Whitchurch, Hurstbourn, and Owslebury estates, and the
rents of the Hospital demesne lands, and the fines on

the renewal of leases. The former, for the year ending Michaelmas, 1835, amounted to £1088. 2s. 9d., which may be classed under the following heads :—

Revenue of the Hospital in 1835.

Reserved rents on leases	£195	7	0
Four small fee-farm rents	1	0	4
Pensions from Churches Exton, £5. 6s. 8d.; Stockbridge, £5; Farley, £1. 6s. 8d.; Baughurst, £1; Bishop's Waltham, £13. 6s. 8d.; Upham, £8; Chilbolton, £2. 13s. 4d.; Nursling, £2; Millbrook, £1. 6s. 8l.; Alverstoke, £6. 13s. 4d.; Ovington, £2; Hinton Ampner, £2; Woodhay, £5; and Alton Canons, £5	59	13	4
Tithes of St. Faith—large, £240; small, £25. 5s.	265	5	0
Hurstbourn, Whitchurch, and Owslebury corn rents	419	12	6
Rent of the Hospital demesne lands	145	0	0
Licence to fish at St. Cross and land-tax of certain tenements	2	4	7
	£1088	2	9

Expenditure of the Hospital in 1835.

The disbursements of the year ending 2nd February, 1836, were as follow :—

To thirteen Brethren, at 1s. each per week ...	£33	6	0
To Hundred Hall poor, 6d. per week to forty persons	52	0	0
Thirteen Brethren for Lent-money in lieu of meat £1. 1s. each	13	13	0
Ditto quarterage, 8s. each	20	16	0
Ditto milk money, 8s. 5d. a quarter	28	17	8
Ditto pan money	0	4	4
Cook's wages	13	0	0
Salary to Chaplain	80	0	0
,, Steward	80	0	0
,, Chaplain of Freefolk	15	0	0
,, Clerk and Porter, £2. 2s. each ...	4	4	0
,, Barber	3	2	0
Allowance to tenants in lieu of customary dinner	2	10	0
Wine for sacrament	4	9	0

	£	s.	d.
Pancakes, Shrove Tuesday, 12s. 6d.; for hens for supper, Shrove Tuesday, 7s.; salt fish, Palm Sunday, 10s. 6d.	1	10	0
Half-pence on six dole days	3	15	10
Washing surplice, £1. 4s.; charcoal, £1. 16s. ...	3	0	0
Faggots	5	0	0
Butcher	137	6	6
Baker, etc.	62	10	10
Coals	15	16	6
Malt and hops	133	5	0
Brewing	8	0	0
Groceries	6	17	1
Labour	14	16	3
Paper, etc.	3	0	0
Land-tax out of pensions from Churches ...	8	12	0
Redeemed land-tax on St. Faith's Rectory, payable to Bishop	12	18	6
Quit-rent to Dean and Chapter for certain lands ...	0	18	4
,, Bishop for water-courses	5	10	8
Collecting Ashton quit-rents	1	15	0
Beer on gaudy days, £1; mince pies, £6. 11s. 8d.	7	11	8
Pensions—to Dean and Chapter, £8. 0s. 8d.; to the Bishop, £1. 2s. 8d.; to the Vicar of Crondall, £6. 13s. 4d.	15	16	8
Abatement on tithes of St. Faith ...	33	15	0
Insurance of Hospital premises ...	1	13	0
Land-tax	0	2	9
Clothing, thirteen Brothers' gowns included	19	10	0
Apothecary's bill	28	12	0
Repairs and incidents	38	11	4
Total disbursements ...	£921	6	11

The last item includes only minor repairs, which are
defrayed by the Steward, whose charge it is to make all
the ordinary payments on account of the Hospital; but as
the funds in his hands are not adequate to meet the
heavier items, they are discharged by the Master.

It appears that the Earl of Guilford had, at the period
when this return was made, expended nearly £6000 in the

repair of the Hospital premises, being on an average more than £200 per annum.

The other source from whence the Hospital derives its income is by fines paid on the renewal of leases, either for lives or years.

III.

During the Mastership of the Earl of Guilford, up to 1836, a period of twenty-eight years, these fines amounted to £41,558. 2s., and arose from the following properties :—

Fines received in the Twenty=eight Years previous to 1836.

Tithes of Aldershot, two renewals, leasehold	... £1000	0	0
,, Itchenswell, one ditto	...	... 424	0	0
,, Hurstbourn and St. Mary Bourne, one ditto	... ...	... 1424	0	0
,, Freefolk, four ditto ...		... 1550	0	0
,, Owslebury, one ditto	...	... 730	0	0
,, Whitchurch (with land), two ditto		... 6595	0	0
,, Fareham, three ditto	...	... 12244	0	0
,, Twyford, one ditto ...	...	... 1200	0	0
,, Long Sutton, three ditto	...	... 2000	0	0
,, St. Cross Mill, three ditto		... 600	0	0
Premises in Winchester, leasehold		... 149	5	0
,, at St. Faith, ditto ...	...	... 833	5	0
,, at Ashton, ditto ...	...	... 200	0	0
,, at Ashton, copyhold ...	...	... 1455	19	0
,, at Whitchurch and Hurstbourn copyhold		960	11	0
		£31366	0	0

Since the above returns were furnished, Crondall and Yately have been renewed for about £12,000, and by the new lease the reserve rents were increased, so as to allow an addition of 1s. a week to each of the Brethren.

IV.
Pay and Maintenance of the Staff.

The payment of the Hospital is thus conducted :—The
Steward is paid a salary of £80 by half-yearly instalments,
and to the Chaplain a similar salary, and £15 as the
Minister of Freefolk Chapel. They also receive 6d. in
the pound on all fines, except those on the copyhold
estates, which are very small. The thirteen Brethren
receive money on every Saturday throughout the year, 1s.
each [recently increased to 2s.], and in lieu of milk, per
quarter 5s. 4d., and also a further quarterly payment of 8s.
each, likewise 2d. each for "pan money" at Michaelmas
and Lady Day. They have also 2d. each in the pound
upon every fine (except upon the copyhold estates) agree-
able to the Consuetudinarium. The whole of the money
payments amount to 2s. 3d. each [now 3s. 3d. each] per
week, from which they provide fuel, washing, and other
requisites, except bread, meat, and beer. They have each
a black gown every Christmas, and bear a silver cross on
the breast.

They are provided with a dinner four days in the
week in the Common Hall, namely, Sunday, Monday,
Tuesday, and Thursday, each taking his share of the
provisions, which are dressed by the cook of the Hospital,
together with the vegetables which they raise in their
separate gardens, into their own chamber. The dinners
are as follow :—On Sunday, three shoulders of mutton or
veal ; on Monday, a neck and leg of mutton ; on Tuesday
and Thursday, boiled beef. The average consumption is
about 100lb. per week. Each Brother has three quarts of
beer per day, and a loaf of about 1½lb. On the gaudy,
or extraordinary days, they have an extra dinner provided
of about 45lb. of roast beef, with mince pies and plum
broth, a jack of beer (containing four gallons), besides 4s.

among them for beer money. A charcoal fire is likewise provided in the Hall by the Master at five o'clock every gaudy day afternoon, when three roast necks of mutton are given them for supper. To the Steward is given 45 lb. of roasting beef annually, in lieu of his share in the gaudy day dinners, also a portion of the mince pies, etc. The Brethren have also a twopenny loaf each on the six dole days. The Master occasionally gives the Brethren an extra dinner, and at Christmas presents them (annually) with six bushels of coals each. When there is a fall of timber, he also gives up the lop and top to them.

V.

The Hundred Hall Poor.

To the poor of the Hundred Hall is paid 26s. each, or 6d. a week at such periods as are found convenient. It frequently happens that a double payment is directed by the Master to be made to one individual. The doles consist of a small loaf, of the value of about 1d., of which five sacks full, or thereabout, are given away to such poor persons as choose to apply, deducting one loaf for each prisoner in the County Gaol at Winchester, to whom it has always been customary to send this relief. When the bread is exhausted, ½d. is given to every applicant who is unsupplied. These are distributed on the Eves of Christmas, Easter, Whitsuntide, and All Saints, the 3rd of May, and the 10th of August.

The ancient custom of relieving the poor travellers who call at the gate is still kept up. A quantity of bread, called a cast, consisting of two loaves of about twenty ounces each, and two gallons of the Hospital beer are provided for the purpose. The whole is now always called for by poor persons before ten o'clock in the morning. Each loaf is cut into about a dozen pieces, one of which is given, with a horn of beer holding not quite half a pint, to each applicant.

After meeting the above expenditure, the whole of the surplus annual rents, the whole of the fines of the copyhold estates, and the fines of the leasehold estates, subject to the deductions of 6*d.* each in the pound to the Steward and Chaplain, and 2*d.* each to the thirteen Brethren, are accounted for by the Steward to the Master.

VI.

Analysis of the Yearly Expenditure.

From this Report it appears that the permanent income of the Hospital in 1836 amounted to £1088. 2*s.* 9*d.*, and sums received on the renewal of leases during a period of twenty-eight years to £41,558, and the disbursements for the year 1836 were £914. 16*s.* 11*d.*, exclusive of extensive repairs for twenty-eight years, which amounted to above £5600. From the gross amount of fines is to be deducted 6*d.* in every pound on the renewal of all leasehold properties to the Steward and Chaplain, and 2*d.* in the pound to each of the Brethren, which will reduce it to £33,433 ; or the annual receipts and expenditure of the Hospital may be thus rendered :—

Annual rents and fixed payments	...	£1088	2	9
Annual average of fines on renewals	...	1484	10	0
		£2572	12	9
Steward's disbursements ...	£914 16 11			
Annual average amount of repairs	200 0 0			
Steward's, Chaplain's, and Brethren's shares of fines	290 7 6			
		1405	4	5
Leaving to the Master the annual average sum of	£1167	8	4

WATER MEADOWS AT ST. CROSS.

Scheme for the Management

OF

The Hospital of St. Cross.

The following is the Scheme, dated 29th January, 1901,
for the administration of the Hospital of St. Cross, including
the Almshouse of Noble Poverty.—Approved by an Order of
the Board of Charity Commissioners.

TRUSTEES.

Trustees and their Qualifications.

1.—The Charity and the property thereof shall be under
the management and control of Trustees, the full number of
whom shall be fifteen.

The Trustees of the Charity shall consist of the Master
of the Hospital, the Dean of Winchester, the Mayor of
Winchester and one other representative of the Winchester
Town Council (if Members of the Church of England), the
Warden of St. Mary's College, Winchester, and the Vicar of
Compton, in the County of Southampton, for the time being
respectively, who shall be *ex-officio* Trustees, and of nine non-
official Trustees, who shall be competent persons, able and
willing to discharge the duties of the trust, resident in the
County of Southampton, and being Members of the Church
of England.

The Representative of the Winchester Town Council, other
than the Mayor, is to be elected by the Town Council from
among their number at a meeting of that body, of which due
notice shall have been given, and he shall be entitled to act as
a Trustee of the Charity for a period of three years from the
date at which the Town Clerk of Winchester formally notifies
to the Clerk of the Trustees that he has been duly elected to
serve as such Representative Trustee.

Appointment.

2.—If any non-official Trustee of the Charity shall become
bankrupt, or compound with his creditors, or become incapacitated to act, or cease to be resident in the County of
Southampton, or to be a Member of the Church of England,
or shall not attend any Meeting of the Trustees during a

H *a*

consecutive period of two years, the Trustees shall cause a record of the fact to be entered in their books, and upon such record being entered the Trustee to whom it applies shall immediately cease to be a Trustee; and thereupon, or upon the death or resignation of any non-official Trustee, a new Trustee qualified as aforesaid shall be appointed by the other Trustees at their first Meeting, which shall be held after the lapse of one calendar month, by a resolution, to be forthwith notified by them, with all proper information, to the Charity Commissioners for England and Wales at their Office in London; but no such appointment shall be valid until it has been approved by the said Commissioners and their approval certified under their Official Seal. No *ex-officio* Trustee shall be allowed to act in the administration of the Charity until he shall have signed a memorandum to the effect that he is a Member of the Church of England, and is willing to undertake the trust as regulated by this Scheme.

As to the Legal Estate.

3.—The Master and Brethren of the Hospital shall permit the Trustees to receive and take the annual and other rents, issues, and profits of all and singular the real estates vested in the Master and Brethren, and from time to time to manage, let, and set the same, and to use, order, and dispose of the goods and personal estate held by the Master and Brethren, in such manner as the Trustees shall in their discretion think best. And, for the purposes aforesaid, the Master and Brethren shall in their corporate capacity make and execute all such deeds, leases, and other instruments, and do and perform all such acts, as the Trustees shall require. The Trustees shall be at liberty to use the corporate name of the Master and Brethren for the purpose of bringing or defending such actions and suits at law and in equity as the Trustees shall think proper and be authorized to do, the Master and Brethren being saved harmless and indemnified therein out of the estates.

Not to hold Charity Property.

4.—None of the Trustees shall at any time, either directly or indirectly, accept a lease of, or hold or occupy the estate and property belonging to the Charity, or any part thereof, or any interest therein, for his own benefit or for the benefit of any person or persons whomsoever.

The Clerk.
Duties and Salary.

5.—The Trustees shall from time to time appoint a fit and proper person to be their Clerk, and may pay to him such stipend as may be approved by the Charity Commissioners. His duties shall be to summon Meetings of the Trustees, and to circulate with the notice of Meeting items of the business to be transacted thereat, to attend such Meetings, and, when so directed, to attend any Committee that may be appointed, to enter the Minutes of the proceedings of Meetings of Trustees in the Minute Book, and to circulate copies thereof amongst the Trustees, to transmit to the Charity Commissioners once in every year a full and detailed account of the receipts and payments of the Charity, to notify to the Charity Commissioners any appointment of a new Trustee with all necessary information, to obtain from every Trustee appointed, and from a Master when appointed, the Declaration required by this Scheme, and to perform such other duties as the Trustees shall direct. The Common Seal belonging to the Master and Brethren shall be kept by the Clerk of the Trustees.

The Receiver.
Duties and Remuneration.

6.—The Trustees may appoint some fit and proper person to be Receiver of the rents and incomes of the Charity Estate, who shall give security for the moneys which may come to his hands and for the due performance of his duty, and shall be remunerated out of the rents and profits of the Charity Estate, provided that such remuneration shall not exceed £5 per cent. per annum on the amount of the rents and profits actually received by him, with an additional £60 per annum and all out-of-pocket expenses in respect of his special duties with regard to the candidates for admission as inmates, and with regard to Pensioners as hereinafter mentioned.

The duties of the Receiver shall be to attend the Trustees at their meetings and to attend and give information to any committee that may be appointed by the Trustees; to collect and get in the rents, profits and income of the Charity Estates and property; to make all disbursements and payments from time to time sanctioned by the Trustees; to keep the accounts of the Charity; to preserve, subject to the direction of the Trustees, all vouchers for payments made by him or the Trustees on behalf of the Charity ; once in every year to make out on behalf of the Trustees a full and detailed account of the receipts and payments of the Charity, and produce the same for the purpose of being audited, and attend the audit thereof with the vouchers, and to prepare the necessary accounts for transmission to the Charity Commissioners in manner directed by the Charitable Trusts Acts or otherwise for the time being by law required; also to prepare quarterly statements of receipts and expenditure for the Finance Committee, to see that the lessees and tenants properly performed their covenants and engagements. He shall keep a register of applicants for appointment, whether as Brethren or Pensioners, and make such inquiries regarding them as may be directed generally or specially by the Trustees, circulate such lists among the Trustees as may from time to time be directed, and shall post the necessary notices of vacancies among the Brethren or in the Pension List as they arise as required by this Scheme. He shall keep a register of all persons appointed to be Pensioners, with the date of their appointments and the date and occasion of every vacancy. He shall pay the stipends to the Brethren and Pensioners, and conduct any inquiries with regard to them. He shall also perform all such other duties as are herein specified or as appertain to his office as the Trustees shall direct.

PORTER.

Salary and Duties.

7.—The Trustees shall appoint some fit and proper person to be Porter at the Hospital, at a salary not exceeding £50 per annum, who shall hold his office during the approbation of the Trustees. The duties of the porter shall be to take charge of the Hospital buildings and premises, and keep the same in a clean and orderly condition.

MEETINGS OF TRUSTEES.

Date and Notice.

8.—The Trustees shall hold not less than four General Meetings in each year for transacting the business of the Charity, which shall be held at such convenient place as the Trustees shall determine, and such meetings shall be held on the days following in each year, that is to say the, second Monday in January, April, July, and October respectively, unless the trustees shall in any year appoint some other days and periods for the holding thereof ; provided, however, that such substituted days of meeting shall be in the same months as aforesaid. And notice of every meeting, whether general or special, shall be given by the Clerk in writing to each Trustee three clear days at the least before the time appointed for holding the same, and such notice may be delivered at the residence of each Trustee, or sent by post.

Quorum, Chairman and Vice-Chairman.

9.—At every meeting any five of the Trustees, so long as there shall be ten or more Trustees, and when there shall be less than ten, any number not being less than one-half the existing body, shall form a quorum. The Trustees may elect a Chairman and Vice-Chairman for their meetings from among their number, and determine the period for which each of them is to hold office, but if no such Chairman or Vice-Chairman is elected, or if at any meeting neither the Chairman nor the Vice-Chairman is present at the time appointed for holding the same, so soon as a sufficient number of Trustees shall be present to form a quorum the Trustees shall proceed to elect for the purpose of that meeting a Chairman from amongst the Trustees present; and, in the event of an equality of votes on the election of Chairman, the question shall be decided between the persons proposed by lot; and the acts and proceedings of a majority of the Trustees present at any meeting properly held shall be binding on the whole body of the Trustees; but the Trustees, or the majority of them, present at any subsequent meeting, duly held and constituted as aforesaid, shall have power from time to time to alter, vary, or rescind any resolution or direction which may have been come to or given at any previous meeting; provided always, that the Chairman of every meeting shall, in the event of an equality of votes at such meeting, have a second or casting vote.

Adjournment.

10.—If at any meeting there shall not, after the space of one hour from the time appointed for holding the same, be a sufficient number of Trustees in attendance to form a quorum, or the business of any meeting shall remain undisposed of, the Trustees, or any one or more of them present at any such meeting, or if no Trustee be present, then the Clerk of the Trustees, may adjourn the same until some subsequent day, of the time and place of holding which three clear days' notice at the least in writing shall be given in manner hereinbefore provided to each Trustee by the Clerk.

Special Meetings.

11.—If at any time any matter shall arise requiring the consideration of the Trustees, which cannot be conveniently deferred to the next General Meeting, any two or more of the Trustees or the Clerk may call a Special Meeting of the Trustees, and the Clerk shall give notice in writing to each of the Trustees of the time and place and object of such meeting, which notice shall be sent by the post or left at the usual place of abode of each Trustee three clear days at least before such Meeting, and no business shall be transacted at such Special Meeting other than such as shall be specified in such notice.

Minute and Account Books.

12.—The Trustees shall provide a minute book, wherein shall be entered a minute of their proceedings at every meeting, which minute shall be signed by the Chairman of the next succeeding meeting. They shall also provide all necessary account books, wherein shall be entered an account of the receipts and payments on behalf of the Charity.

BANKERS AND CHEQUES.
Bankers.

13.—The Trustees shall appoint as their banker, during pleasure, some fit and responsible person or persons who is or are carrying on the business of banker, or some Joint Stock Banking Company in the City of Winchester, with whom shall be deposited the moneys of the Charity.

Signature of Cheques.

14.—All cheques and orders for the payment of money shall be signed either at a meeting of Trustees by the Chairman of the meeting and by two of the other Trustees present at such meeting, and shall be countersigned by the Clerk, or if out of meeting they shall be signed by the

Chairman or Vice-Chairman elected for a period under Clause 9 hereof and by two other Trustees, and shall be countersigned by the Clerk.

CUSTODY OF DOCUMENTS.
Box to be Provided.

15.—The Trustees shall procure for themselves out of the funds of the charity one or more fire-proof box or boxes, with two keys and a secure lock, which shall be deposited in such secure place within the Hospital as they shall direct : and in which box or boxes shall be deposited an office copy of this scheme, and of the certificate approving thereof, and the vouchers, accounts, books, deeds, writings, manuscripts, and other documents, belonging to the charity, together with a list in writing thereof signed by the Clerk, and such box or boxes shall be kept locked, and one key thereof be kept by the Clerk and the other by such one of the Trustees as the majority of them present at any meeting shall direct. The list of the contents shall be verified once a year in the month of October by the Clerk and one of the Trustees appointed for the purpose. No document shall be lent except under special circumstances on conditions approved by the Trustees.

16.—The Trustees shall provide a fire-proof box, wherein shall be deposited the Registers of Baptisms, Burials, and Marriages, and such box shall be kept in some secure place within the Hospital in the custody and under the control of the Master.

POWERS AND DUTIES OF TRUSTEES.
Leases.

17.—The lands and buildings of the Charity (except the buildings within the precincts of the Hospital) shall from time to time be let and demised at the best annual rent or rents that can reasonably be obtained for the same, either from year to year, or for any term or number of years not exceeding twenty-one years in possession, and not in reversion, and without taking any fine or premium on the making of any such demise, but the surrender of any existing term not having more than three years to run shall not be considered as a premium; and on the granting of any lease the lessee shall execute a counterpart of the lease. All leases shall contain covenants on the part of the lessee for the due payment of the rent, the proper cultivation of the land, the repair and insurance of the houses and buildings comprised therein, a proviso for re-entry on non-payment of rent or non-performance of covenants and all other usual and proper covenants applicable to the property which shall be the subject of the lease.

Allotments.

18.—The Trustees may set apart and let in allotments, in the manner prescribed by and subject to the provisions of the Allotments Extension Act, 1882, any portions of the land belonging to the Charity other than buildings and the appurtenances of buildings.

Hospital to be kept in Repair and Insured.

19.—The Trustees shall keep the Hospital Buildings and Premises, including the House allocated to the Master for the time being, in good and sufficient repair, and sufficiently insured against damage by fire; and the expenses thereof, and of the rates and taxes, if any, shall be paid out of the income of the Charity.

Fabric Fund.

20.—The Trustees shall be at liberty to set apart the sum of £6000 as a Building Fund, which shall be available for maintaining the Church of St. Cross, the Hospital Buildings, and the Chancels of Churches for which the Trustees are responsible as Rectors, in proper repair, and to allow the interest to accumulate, and they shall be at liberty to supplement the same by an annual sum not exceeding £500 out of the surplus income until the Fund amounts to £10,000. When the Fund amounts to this sum the interest shall be appropriated for the general purposes of the Charity, but whenever any expenditure is charged to the Fund the interest shall again be accumulated until the Fund is brought up to the sum of £10,000.

Expenses of Church.

21.—The Trustees shall, out of the income of the Charity, ake all such payments as may be necessary for the due and derly performance of Divine Service at the Church of St. Cross.

COMMITTEES.

Power to Appoint.

22.—It shall be lawful for the Trustees at any General or Special Meeting, to nominate and appoint from their own body, as there may be occasion, three or more Trustees to be a Committee, for the purpose of making any inquiry or super-intending any duty, which, in the judgment of the Trustees, would be more efficiently executed by such Committee; but the acts and proceedings of such Committee shall be submitted to the Trustees at their next General Meeting for approval and confirmation.

Visiting Committee.

23.—The Trustees shall, once or oftener in every year, at one of their meetings, nominate three or more persons from their body as a Committee to visit the Hospital and to view the state and condition thereof, and to hear and take cognizance of any complaint or complaints by the inmates thereof, touching the management thereof, and such Committee shall report any grievances brought to their attention to the Trustees at their next general meeting, or, if necessary, at a special meeting to be called for the purpose.

To Report Annually.

24.—The persons forming such Committee shall annually make a report in writing to the Trustees of the state and condition of the Hospital, and any special matter relating thereto brought to their knowledge, which report shall be entered by the Clerk in the minute book of proceedings, and shall be signed by the persons forming such Committee.

THE MASTER.
Appointment.

25.—The Master of the Hospital shall be a clergyman of the Church of England in priest's orders, and the appointment of the Master shall be in the Bishop of Winchester for the time being, and such Master shall be subject in all respects to the jurisdiction of the said Bishop as Ordinary.

Stipend and Allowances.

26.—The Trustees shall pay to every future Master of the Hospital a fixed annual stipend of £250, and they shall make to him a further annual payment of £150, subject, however, to the following condition, namely, that if in any year the Master is, in the opinion of the Trustees, incapacitated from any cause for the due performance of his duties, the Trustees may, with the written consent of the Lord Bishop of Win-

chester, and after not less than six calendar months' notice to
the Master, withhold either wholly or in part the payment of
the said annual sum of £150. They shall also be at liberty to
pay to the Master if and so long as they shall think fit the
further sum of not more than £100 per annum, to be applied by
him towards providing a salary for any Assistant Minister or
Curate who may be employed to assist the Master in the
discharge of his duties in relation to the Church of St. Cross
and the Parish of St. Faith, provided that any such Assistant
Minister shall be on the footing of a Licensed Curate in and
for the Parish of St. Faith, and shall be subject to all the
incidents of that position.

The annual stipend of £400 shall be continued to the
present Master of the Hospital, with the additional payment,
if the Trustees think fit, of £100 per annum to be applied as
aforesaid, subject in all respects to the same conditions on
which the said sums have heretofore been paid.

If at any time the Master shall desire to resign his appointment upon any of the grounds mentioned for resigning a
Benefice in the Incumbents Resignation Act, 1871, the
Trustees may in such case, upon being satisfied that such
grounds exist, award him, upon his vacating the house allotted
to him, a pension for life from the revenues of the Hospital
not exceeding with any pension he may be allowed under the
said Act, the sum of £200 per annum. Provided that in the
case of the present Master he may be permitted to occupy the
house, garden, and premises now in his occupation.

Residence.

27.—Every future Master of the Hospital shall reside in
and occupy the house recently erected for the use of future
Masters, with such garden or gardens as may from time to
time be allotted by the Trustees, but shall not underlet, demise,
or assign over the same, nor be entitled to occupy any
other part of the lands belonging to the Charity. And if
in any year the Master is, in the opinion of the Trustees,
incapacitated from any cause for the due performance of his
duties the Trustees may, with the written consent of the Lord
Bishop of Winchester, give not less than six calendar months'
notice to the Master to vacate the house and garden so allotted,
and at the expiration of such notice the Master shall vacate
and deliver over possession of the same to the Trustees.

The present Master shall be allowed to reside in and occupy the house and gardens now in his occupation, subject in all respects to the same conditions on which they have heretofore been held by him.

To have General Management of Hospital.

28.—The Master shall have the government and control of the Hospital under the general superintendence of the Trustees.

Duties.

29.—The Master shall read Prayers every morning, and perform two full services every Sunday, in the Church of St. Cross, according to the ritual of the Church of England, and shall perform one full service there once at least on every Christmas Day, Good Friday, and day of Public Fast or Thanksgiving. He shall also visit the inmates of the Hospital in sickness and otherwise, as there shall be occasion. He shall also perform, with reference to the parishioners and inhabitants of the parish of St. Faith, in the churchyard and elsewhere in the said parish, all the usual duties of an incumbent towards the parishioners and inhabitants of his parish, and shall not be entitled to take any fees from any inmates, parishioners, and inhabitants. He shall keep the Registers of Baptisms, Burials, and Marriages, and shall transmit copies of the same in such manner as Incumbents of parishes are required by law to do.

To keep a Register of Brethren.

30.—The Trustees shall provide a Register, in which the Master shall enter the names and age of every man elected into the Hospital, together with the date of his admission thereto, and the state of health, place of residence and condition in life of every such man previous to his election.

St. Cross Church.
The Church of St. Cross.

31.—The Church of St. Cross shall be open to all persons at the time of Divine Service; and, after providing therein for the due accommodation of the inmates of the Hospital, all the sittings shall be free: provided always, that in arranging the accommodation to be given to persons attending at the Church, preference shall be given to the Parishioners of St.

Faith. The Trustees shall be at liberty, upon application
being made to them for the purpose, and during their pleasure,
to allot, according to the capacity of the Church, certain
sittings for the use of such of the Parishioners of St. Faith as
may be regular attendants at the Church.

Clerk and Sexton.

32.—The Trustees shall appoint some fit and proper person
to perform the usual and necessary duties of Clerk and Sexton
in the Church of St. Cross, and in the Churchyard of St.
Faith, and may allow him for his trouble any sum not
exceeding £10 per annum.

Freefolk Chapel.

33.—The Trustees shall pay a yearly sum of £80 to the
Clergyman for the time being officiating at the Chapel of
Freefolk, and may, if they think fit, pay him a further yearly
sum of not more than £40.

PATRONAGE OF ALDERSHOT.
Transfer of Advowson.

34.—The Trustees shall be at liberty to effect, in accordance with the provisions of any Scheme which may be
prepared by the Ecclesiastical Commissioners for England,
a Transfer and Assignment to the Bishop of the Diocese
of Winchester for the time being of the Advowson or
perpetual right of Patronage of and presentation to the
Church and Cure of St. Michael's, Aldershot.

Power to Exchange the Whitchurch Rectory House.

35.—The Trustees of the said Charity shall be at liberty
to effect an exchange with the Vicar of Whitchurch, with
the consent of the Bishop of the Diocese and Patron of the
Living of Whitchurch, of the present Rectory House and
adjoining lands, containing 3 acres, 2 roods, 30 poles,
belonging to the Charity for the Vicarage House of Whitchurch and adjoining lands, containing 2 roods, 9 poles,
belonging to that Vicarage, and without any pecuniary or
other consideration.

BRETHREN.
Two Classes.

36.—There shall be two classes of Brethren to be maintained in manner hereinafter prescribed, the Brethren of the

Hospital of St. Cross, and the Brethren of the Almshouse of Noble Poverty.

Number.

As many Brethren of the two classes may from time to time be appointed as the Hospital buildings and the funds at the disposal of the Trustees may suffice to receive and maintain, provided that the number of the Brethren of the Hospital of St. Cross shall never be less than thirteen.

Additional Rooms.

37.—The Trustees may adapt at a cost not exceeding £1500 the Master's House in the quadrangle for ten or more sets of rooms for Brethren in addition to the existing seventeen sets of rooms.

Appropriation of Rooms.

38.—Of the twenty-seven sets of rooms eighteen shall be allotted for the Brethren of the Hospital of St. Cross, and shall be attributed to the Hospital Foundation, and nine shall be allotted to Brethren of the Almshouse of Noble Poverty, and shall be attributed to the Noble Poverty Foundation.

Qualification for Hospital Foundation.

39.—The Brethren on the Foundation of the Hospital of St. Cross shall be poor men who shall have attained the age of sixty-five years at the least, who shall not have been in receipt of parochial relief within twelve months next preceding the time of election, and who shall be so reduced in strength as not to be able to work.

Qualification for Noble Poverty Foundation.

40.—The Brethren on the Foundation of the Almshouse of Noble Poverty shall be poor men who shall have attained the age of sixty years at the least, who shall not have been in receipt of parochial relief within twelve months next preceding the time of election, and who shall have been reduced by misfortune from independence to poverty.

Cases of Exceptional Infirmity.

41.—Provided that in any case of exceptional infirmity the Trustees may elect a person otherwise duly qualified who shall be above the age of fifty-five to be a Brother of the

Hospital of St. Cross or of the Almshouse of Noble Poverty. In such case the reason for making the exception shall be recorded in the minute book.

Election.

42.—On the occasion of any vacancy among the Brethren. the Trustees shall elect a person, duly qualified as aforesaid, The Trustees shall not in rotation appoint or elect persons to supply any such vacancy nor make any other arrangements, so as to convert such appointment to private patronage, but shall elect such person as shall, after a careful consideration of the claims of the several candidates, appear to be most deserving.

Stipends, Allowances, and Gowns.

43.—The stipends in money of the Brethren of the Hospital shall be 10s. a week each. All allowances and distributions of food now made shall for the present be continued. The Trustees shall, once in each year, at Christmas time, give to each of the Brethren a cloth gown; and the Brethren shall at all times appear in such gowns.

Power to vary Allowances.

44.—The Trustees shall be at liberty, if they shall think fit, to abolish the system of supplying the Brethren with food, and of making certain payments and allowances to them as hereinbefore provided, and shall in such case pay to each of them a certain fixed stipend, not exceeding £50 per annum, by weekly instalments, in lieu of all such allowances and payments, excepting the gowns as aforesaid; but such altera-tions shall not be made so as to affect any of the Brethren appointed prior to the 10th day of March, 1874, without their consent.

To attend Service.

45.—The Brethren shall, unless prevented by sickness, attend all the services performed in the Church of St. Cross.

Not to Sub-let.

46.—The Brethren shall not be permitted to let the rooms allotted to them in the Hospital, or any part thereof, nor to allow any stranger to occupy the same.

Not to Absent Themselves.

47.—The Brethren shall not absent themselves from the Hospital at night without special leave first obtained from the Master.

Power to Remove Brethren.

48.—If at any time it shall happen that any of the Brethren now or hereafter to be appointed or elected to the Hospital shall be given to insobriety, or immoral, insubordinate, or unbecoming conduct, the Trustees shall, upon proof thereof to their satisfaction, or upon the report of any Committee appointed for the purpose of investigating the matter, if they shall see fit, displace such person or persons so misbehaving, and another or others shall be elected in his or their place or places in manner hereinbefore directed. The provisions of this clause shall be made known to each of the Brethren.

MEDICAL ATTENDANCE.
Doctor.

49.—The Trustees shall be at liberty to expend such a sum, not exceeding £30 per annum, or such further sum as may be approved by the Charity Commissioners, as will procure medical attendance and all necessary medicines for the Brethren when sick.

Nurse.

50.—The Trustees shall also be at liberty to appoint a duly qualified person to act as Nurse, and to attend upon the Brethren in case of illness or infirmity. A separate set of rooms may be assigned to the Nurse within the Hospital rent free, and the Trustees shall be at liberty to pay to her such reasonable weekly wages out of the income of the Charity as they shall think fit. An additional Nurse or Nurses may also be employed by the Trustees in special cases of emergency, upon such terms of remuneration as the Trustees may determine.

PENSIONS.
Appropriation.

51.—Subject to the before mentioned payments and allowances to be made to the Brethren, the Trustees shall apply a portion of the income of the Charity in the maintenance of pensions as follows :—

	Yearly charge.		
	£	s	d
(a) Twenty-four pensions at the rate of 8s. a week each for single men or women qualified under Clauses 52 or 53. ...	499	4	0
(b) Pensions to be attributed to the Hospital Foundation :—			
Eighteen pensions at the rate of £26 a year each for 18 married couples	468	0	0
(c) Pensions to be attributed to the Noble Poverty Foundation :—			
Four pensions at the rate of £40 a year each for four married couples	160	0	0
Four pensions at the rate of £26 a year each for single men or women	104	0	0

Qualification for Hospital Foundation.

52.—Pensioners on the Foundation of the Hospital of St. Cross shall be poor persons who shall not have been in receipt of parochial relief within twelve months next preceding the time of election, who shall be so reduced in strength as not to be able to work, and who shall have attained the age of sixty-five years at the least. Provided always that in the case of pensions to married couples it shall be sufficient if the husband has attained the age of sixty-five years.

Qualification for Noble Poverty Foundation.

53.—Pensioners on the Foundation of the Almshouse of Noble Poverty shall be poor persons, who shall not have been in receipt of parochial relief within twelve months next preceding the time of election, who shall have been reduced by misfortune from independence to poverty, and who shall have attained the age of sixty years at the least. Provided always that in the case of pensions to married couples it shall be sufficient if the husband has attained the age of sixty years.

Cases of Exceptional Infirmity.

54.—Provided that in any case of exceptional infirmity the Trustees may elect a person otherwise duly qualified who shall be above the age of fifty-five to be a Pensioner on either Foundation. In such case the reason for making the exception shall be recorded in the Minute Book.

APPENDIX.

Reduced and Limited Pensions

55.—The Trustees in lieu of granting full pensions may grant a larger number at reduced rates, but no diversion of the amounts appropriated to each Foundation shall be made and no pension shall be granted of a less amount than 5s. weekly. The Trustees, in lieu of paying the whole amount of the stipend to any pensioner in money, may from time to time expend the whole or any portion thereof for his or her benefit as they think fit. In the case of Pensioners of any of the aforesaid classes possessing, at the date of appointment or afterwards, a properly secured income from other sources or being in receipt of assistance from relations or others amounting to less than the stipend allowed in that class, the Trustees may pay the full stipend or a portion thereof, provided that the total income shall not amount to more than—

In Class (a), 15s. a week ;

   ,,   (b), £40 a year ;

   ,,   (c), £50 a year for married couples, and £40 a year for single persons.

Pensions for Widows of Brothers and Widows or Widowers of Pensioners.

56.—On the death of a married Brother or Pensioner (being the survivor of a married couple pensioned under Clause 51) the Trustees may in their discretion award to the widow of a Brother or to the widow or widower of such Pensioner whether qualified under Clause 52 or Clause 53 or not, if on the Hospital Foundation, a pension not exceeding 8s. a week, and to the widow of a Brother or to the widow or widower of such Pensioner, whether qualified under one of the said clauses or not, if on the Noble Poverty Foundation, a pension not exceeding £26 a year; provided that no such pension shall be at less rate than 5s. a week. Such pensions shall be attributed in the case of the widow of an inmate on the Hospital Foundation to the pensions authorised by Clause 51 (a) and in the case of the widow or widower of a Pensioner on the Hospital Foundation, to the pensions authorised by Clause 51 (b), and in the case of the widow of an inmate, or the widow or widower of a Pensioner on the Noble Poverty Foundation, to the pensions authorised by Clause 51 (c).

H b

Restriction in case of Pensions awarded under last Clause.

57.—If the Trustees award under the last Clause a pension to the widow of a Brother or a Pensioner, or to the widower of a Pensioner, no vacancy occurring in the number of the like class of pensions, under Clause 51, shall be filled up until the amount awarded in pensions in such class is reduced below the amount authorised by Clause 51, unless the Trustees are satisfied the income of the Charity will suffice to meet the pensions so awarded, in addition to the pensions authorised by Clause 51.

ELECTION OF PENSIONERS.
Notice and Application.

58.—Subject as herein provided, notice of vacancies and application for appointment as Brethren or Pensioners shall be given and made, and elections shall be conducted, in accordance with rules to be made from time to time by the Trustees, with the approval of the Charity Commissioners.

Appointment.

59.—Every appointment of a Pensioner shall be made by the Trustees at a meeting, of which due notice shall be given to every trustee, and shall be made as soon as conveniently may be after an interval of one month from the occurrence of the vacancy to be filled up, allowing a reasonable time for publication of notice and for inquiries as to the applicants.

Conditions.

60.—The pensions shall be awarded after full investigation of the character and circumstances of the applicants, and inquiry whether they have shown reasonable providence, and whether and to what extent they may reasonably expect assistance from relations or others.

The pensions shall be paid subject to such reasonable regulations for ascertaining the identity and good conduct of the Pensioners and their continued possession of the required qualifications as the Trustees from time to time prescribe.

For the purposes of this clause the Trustees may, if they think fit, avail themselves of the agency of any Charity Organisation Society, or other like agency.

Notice of Vacancies.

61.—Notice of each vacancy, as it occurs, and of the meeting of the Trustees at which it will be filled, shall be put up at the gates of the Hospital.

Elections.

62.—The elections shall be made by the Trustees as a Body, and not by individual Trustees by rotation or otherwise.

Proposal of Candidates.

63.—No candidate shall be voted for unless proposed by one of the Trustees present at the election, or, if absent, by letter addressed by him to the Chairman.

Pension Committee.

64.—The Trustees may appoint a committee to examine the list of candidates, and to recommend those whom they consider to be the most deserving ; but this shall not preclude any Trustee from proposing for election a candidate who may not be recommended by the committee.

Candidates' Information.

65.—A list of all the Candidates, with their addresses, and information of their ages and circumstances, shall be circulated to the Trustees, and whenever any addition is made to the list of candidates, such addition shall be circulated in like manner.

OTHER REGULATIONS AS TO PENSIONS.

When on a Vacancy for a Brother of Noble Poverty Applicant prefers Pension.

66.—In the case of a vacancy in one of the sets of rooms allotted to the Noble Poverty Foundation, if an applicant is chosen who prefers to be a Pensioner, the Trustees may, if funds permit, instead of appointing him to the set of rooms, award him a pension in accordance with the scale laid down in Clause 51 (c), although there may be no vacancy in such pensions, and the vacant set of rooms may be filled by the appointment of a Brother from the list of candidates for rooms allotted to the Hospital Foundation. In such case, as vacancies occur in the Pensions attributed to the Hospital Foundation, a transfer shall be made of £50 a year from the yearly sum for pensions attributed to that Foundation to the yearly sum for pensions attributed to the Noble Poverty Foundation.

Term of.

67.—Each pension shall be granted for a term of three years in the first instance, but may be prolonged by the Trustees, if they think fit, for a further period of not more than three years at each prolongation.

Register.

68.—The Trustees shall provide and keep a book in which shall be entered the name, age, and description of every person appointed to be a Pensioner, and the date of every appointment, and the date and occasion of every vacancy. They shall also keep a register of all applications for appointment.

Removal of Pensioners.

69.—Any Pensioner who receives Poor-law relief shall be removed from being a Pensioner. If in the opinion of the Trustees, any Pensioner is guilty of insobriety, or immoral, or unbecoming conduct, or becomes disqualified for retaining his or her appointment by becoming entitled to a sufficient income from sources other than the Charity, or from any other cause, or if in any case it appears that any Pensioner has been appointed without having the required qualifications, the Trustees, upon proof thereof to their satisfaction, may remove the Pensioner. Upon the removal of any Pensioner the Trustees may proceed to appoint another Pensioner in his or her place. In any case of such misconduct as aforesaid the Trustees may suspend the payment of the stipend to the Pensioner, either wholly or in part, during such time as they think fit. Any pensioner removed on account of receiving Poor-law relief while being detained under lawful authority as a person suffering from mental disease, may, on recovery, be re-appointed without previous notice being given of the vacancy to be filled up, and need not possess the qualifications as to residence and previous non-receipt of Poor-law relief.

Regulations.

70.—The Trustees may from time to time prescribe such reasonable regulations as they consider expedient for the government of the Pensioners, provided that the same shall not be at variance or inconsistent with any of the provisions of this Scheme.

SURPLUS INCOME.
Improvement of Hospital Buildings.

71.—The Trustees shall be at liberty from time to time, with the previous sanction of the Charity Commissioners, to be expressed in an Order of the Board under their official seal, to expend out of the unappropriated surplus income of the Charity such sum or sums as shall be deemed by the Commissioners sufficient, in adding to or otherwise improving the present Hospital buildings in accordance with plans and specifications which shall have been submitted to the Commissioners for their approval, so as to provide additional rooms for the residence of Brethren, or for increasing the number of pensions.

Application of Surplus Income.

72.—The Trustees, after making the several payments hereinbefore directed to be made, and providing for the necessary expenses and outgoings of the current year, shall, at the expiration of each year remit the surplus income of the Charity to "The Official Trustees of Charitable Funds," to be invested in the name of the said Official Trustees in 2½ per Centum Annuities, or in any other of the investments (except mortgages) authorised by the Trustee Act, 1893, or any statutory modification thereof for the investment of Trust Funds.

QUESTIONS UNDER SCHEME.
Construction of Scheme.

73.—Any question as to the construction of this Scheme, or as to the regularity or the validity of any acts done or about to be done under this Scheme, shall be determined conclusively by the Charity Commissioners, upon such application made to them for the purpose, as they think sufficient.

SCHEME TO BE PRINTED.
Trustees and Master to have Copies.

74.—This scheme shall be printed, and a copy thereof given to every person on his appointment as a Trustee or

Master; and every Master shall, on accepting and before entering on the duties of his office, by writing, signed at the foot of one of such printed copies (to be kept by the Trustees), certify that he has read the same, and that he undertakes and agrees to conform to and comply with and be bound by the provisions thereof, so far as the same apply to the office accepted by him.

Trustees of the Hospital of St. Cross.

GENERAL INDEX.

1

THE CITY CROSS WINCHESTER.

[Said to have been built by Cardinal Beaufort.]

LIST OF BOOKS, Etc.

Printed and Published by

WARREN & SON, WINCHESTER.

AN ACCOUNT of some of the FAMILIES bearing the Name of HEATHCOTE, which have descended out of the County of Derby, by EVELYN D. HEATHCOTE, M.A., late Rector of Lainston and Vicar of Sparsholt, in the County of Southampton : 41 fine plates, 150 crests, 31 pedigrees, 280 pp. demy quarto, on superfine paper, half-bound in best vellum. Price £2. 2s. net. Only 200 copies printed.

THE DAWN OF REVELATION. Old Testament Lessons for Teachers in Secondary Schools. By M. BRAMSTON, Author of "Judæa and Her Rulers," etc. With Preface by REV. THE HON. E. LYTTELTON, Head Master of Haileybury College, (xiv + 308 pp.). Crown 8vo, cloth. Price 5s. net.

THE GREAT SCREEN OF WINCHESTER CATHEDRAL. By G. W. KITCHIN, D.D., F.S.A., Dean of Durham. Revised and completed by W. R. W. STEPHENS, B.D., Dean of Winchester ; with Appendix, shewing the Reparations to the Nave Vaulting and Roofs ; over forty fine Illustrations. Demy 4to, 2s. 9d. post free.

THE HAMPSHIRE OBSERVER, the only Penny Paper printed and published in Winchester. Advertisements inserted at Special Rates. Published every Saturday morning at 7 o'clock ; Second Edition at 4 p.m. Proprietors, WARREN & SON, Winchester.

THE HAMPSHIRE HERALD, ALTON GAZETTE, NORTH AND EAST HANTS ADVERTISER. Has the largest circulation in these Districts. Published at the OFFICE, MARKET STREET, ALTON. Price 1d.

Publications by Warren & Son, Winchester.

WINCHESTER DIOCESAN CHRONICLE. A Monthly Record of Church Work in the Diocese. Published with the sanction of the Bishop. Price Twopence, or post free Two Shillings per annum.

COMPOTUS ROLLS OF THE OBEDIENTARIES OF ST. SWITHUN'S PRIORY, WINCHESTER (xiv + 540 pp.). Edited by the VERY REV. G. W. KITCHIN, D.D., F.S.A. Dean of Durham. Published at 21s. net.

WINCHESTER CATHEDRAL MSS., Vol. I ; relating to the Establishment of the Capitular Body of Winchester, A.D. 1541–1547 (217 pp.). Edited by the VERY REV. G. W. KITCHIN, D.D., F.S.A., and the REV. F. T. MADGE, M.A. Published at 10s. 6d. net.

WINCHESTER CATHEDRAL DOCUMENTS, Volume II ; relating to the History of the Cathedral Church, 1636–1683. Edited by the DEAN OF WINCHESTER, B.D., F.S.A., and the REV. F. T. MADGE, M.A. Published at 15s. net.

NUNNA-MINSTER, OR ABBEY OF ST. MARY, WINCHESTER. This MS. is assigned to the Eighth Century, and contains the Passion of our Lord, Prayers, Hymns, etc., and the boundaries of the lands of the Abbey in Winchester, as held at the time of its foundation by St. Ealhswith, with a facsimile page in autotype photography (152 pp.). Edited by W. DE GRAY BIRCH, F.S.A., of the MSS. Department, British Museum. Published at 12s. 6d. net.

RECORDS OF THE MANOR OF CRONDALL, Vol. I ; Historical and Manorial (xxvii + 530 pp.). Edited by F. J. BAIGENT. Published at 21s. net.

EPISCOPAL REGISTER OF BISHOP WILLIAM OF WYKEHAM. Vol. I (1367–1404). Edited by T. F. KIRBY, M.A., F.S.A., Bursar of Winchester College. (xii + 424 pp.) Published at 21s. net.

WYKEHAM'S REGISTER, Vol. II. Edited by T. F. KIRBY, M.A., F.S.A. (xii + 647). Published at 21s. net.

EPISCOPAL REGISTERS (*in extenso*) OF JOHN DE SANDALE AND RIGAUD DE ASSERIO, Bishops of Winchester, A.D. 1316–1323. Edited by FRANCIS JOSEPH BAIGENT. (civ + lxiv + 700 pp.) Published at 21s. net.

CHARTERS AND DOCUMENTS RELATING TO SEL-
BORNE AND ITS PRIORY (xiv + 177 pp.) Edited by
W. DUNN MACRAY, M.A., F.S.A., Fellow of Magd. Coll., Oxford, and
Rector of Ducklington. Published at 12s. 6d. net.

CHARTERS AND DOCUMENTS RELATING TO SEL-
BORNE PRIORY, Second Series (125 pp.) Edited by the
REV. W. D. MACRAY, M.A., of the Bodleian Library. Published at
10s. 6d. net.

THE HYDE REGISTER (xcvi + 335 pp.) Edited by W. DE
GRAY BIRCH, F.S.A., of the MSS. Department, British Museum
Published at 12s. 6d. net.

THE MANOR OF MANYDOWN, HAMPSHIRE (240 pp.)
Edited by the VERY REV. G. W. KITCHIN, D.D., F.S.A., Dean
of Durham. Published at 15s. net.

LIFE OF BISHOP WILLIAM OF WYKEHAM. By REV.
G. H. MOBERLY, M.A. New and Revised Edition, with
Preface by the LORD BISHOP OF SOUTHWELL, and Plates from
CHANDLER'S MS. Demy 8vo. Cash price 5s. post free.

THE HOUSE OF ATREUS: being the Agamemnon, Libation
Bearers, and Furies of Æschylus. Translated into English
Verse by E. D. A. MORSHEAD, M.A. Crown 8vo, cloth, 230 pp.
5s. net.

THE PROMETHEUS BOUND OF AESCHYLUS: Trans-
lated into English Verse by E. D. A. MORSHEAD, M.A., formerly
Fellow of New College, Oxford; Assistant Master of Winchester
College. Crown 8vo, cloth, 76 pp. 2s. net.

NOCTES SHAKSPERIANÆ. A series of Papers by Late and
Present Members of the Winchester College Shakspere Society.
Demy 8vo, 300 pp. 5s. net.

HISTORY OF THE FIRST VOLUNTEER BATTALION
HAMPSHIRE REGIMENT. By COLONEL T. STURMY
CAVE. Crown 8vo, cloth, profusely illustrated, 5s. net, and a few large
paper copies, 10s. 6d. net.

A MEMENTO OF THE ANTIENT AND CHARITABLE SOCIETIES OF NATIVES AND ALIENS. By ALFRED BOWKER, Honorary Secretary to both Societies. Crown 4to, numerous portraits and illustrations, cloth. 10s. 6d. net. (In the press).

SHORT HISTORY AND DESCRIPTION OF THE TOWN OF ALTON, by WM. CURTIS, M.R.C.S., L.S.A. Demy 8vo., 190 pp., 21 plates. Cloth. Published at 6s. net.

THE REAL PRESENCE IN THE EUCHARIST, as taught by the Prayer Book : by the REV. ED. HUNTINGFORD, D.C.L., Hon. Canon of Winchester Cathedral. Price 2d.

THOUGHTS REGARDING THE FUTURE STATE OF ANIMALS. Collected from various sources, by the REV. JOHN FREWEN MOOR, M.A., late Vicar of Ampfield. Second edition, illustrated and enlarged, edited by EDITH CARRINGTON. Crown 8vo, 2s. 9d. net, post free.

READINGS TO THE SICK, by F. P. WICKHAM, M.A., late Rector, Stoke Abbott, Dorset. Crown 8vo., cloth, 2s. net, post free.

DANIEL AND ST. JOHN. Lectures delivered in The Close, Winchester, by REV. CANON HUNTINGFORD, D.D. 8vo, stiff paper, 207 pp. 2s. net.

CHURCHWARDENS' MANUAL: Their Duties, Rights, and Privileges. By THE RT. REV. BISHOP SUMNER. Revised and Enlarged with special reference to the Burial Laws, the Position of District Churches, and the Conveyance of Land or Buildings for Trust purposes. F'cap. 8vo, cloth, 1s. 6d. net.

HINTS TO CHOIRS AND CHOIRMASTERS. By WILLIAM HENRY DOODY, Lay Vicar of Winchester Cathedral, and Choirmaster of North Hants Choral Union. Crown 8vo, cloth, 1s. 6d.

HYMNS ADAPTED TO THE SEASONS OF THE CHRISTIAN YEAR, Collated and Edited by REV. E. T. HOARE, M.A., Vicar of Chilworth, Hants. Demy 16mo, 480 pp., 1s. 9d. post free.

LYRICS OF THE WHITE CITY (WINCHESTER), by HERBERT POWELL. Crown 8vo., 72 pp., cloth, 2s. 6d. net.

KING ALFRED'S WINCHESTER, by FLORENCE A. G. DAVIDSON, 34 pp. crown 8vo., with 12 illustrations, on art paper. Price 4*d*., or post free 5*d*.

A SHORT ACCOUNT of THE ANCIENT WEST GATE of the City of Winchester ; compiled from the Coffer Books and other Documents found in the Ancient Chest kept within the Gate. By WILLIAM HENRY JACOB, Alderman of the City. With Illustrations. Crown 8vo, 39 pp., 4½*d*., post free.

ENTIRELY NEW EDITION OF WARREN'S SIXPENNY GUIDE TO WINCHESTER. 120 pages ; 50 illustrations ; foolscap 8vo.

SHILLING TOURIST'S GUIDE for the whole District, with Map and Illustrations.

WARREN'S NEW SIXPENNY BOOK OF VIEWS OF WINCHESTER.

POST CARDS, with 12 Vignette VIEWS OF WINCHESTER. 4*d*. per dozen, post free ; printed in tint on best ivory cardboard.

NEW TOURIST'S MAP OF FIFTEEN MILES ROUND WINCHESTER, reduced from the Ordnance Survey, ¾-inch Scale to Mile, with One Mile Radial Lines. Price 1*s*. On Cloth, with Roller, 3*s*.

WINCHESTER AND DISTRICT DIRECTORY, with 150 NEIGHBOURING PLACES and TWO MAPS ; also complete List of Magistrates for the County, County Councillors and Aldermen. Price 1*s*., by post 1*s*. 3*d*. Published in January of each year.

WARREN'S WINCHESTER AND DISTRICT RAILWAY TIME TABLES, with Railway Map and complete List of Fares. Published Monthly, price 1*d*.

SCRIPTURE CARDS. WINCHESTER BIBLE READINGS, 1899. Two Courses, Senior and Junior. 1*d*. each, 10*d*. dozen, 6*s*. per hundred--post free if the order is prepaid.

SYLLABUS OF RELIGIOUS INSTRUCTION for use in the Diocese of Winchester. Second Edition. Post free 4½d., or three copies 1/-

HOLY MARRIAGE: a Booklet printed in Gold.—A Gift Book for the Upper Classes. Price 6d., post free.

HOME LIFE.-- By MRS. SUMNER. Second edition. Crown 8vo., 170 pp., 2s. 6d. post free.

PREPARATION FOR HOLY COMMUNION FOR MOTHERS. Price 2½d. post free.

NURSERY TRAINING: a book for Nurses of Little Children. By MRS. SUMNER. Second edition. Square 12mo, cloth, 63 pp. 1s. net.

TO MOTHERS OF THE HIGHER CLASSES. Second edition. Fcap. 8vo, cloth, 88 pp. 1s. net.

THE VOICE OF THE HOURS, being words arranged to the Westminster Chimes. Cards, with music, 3d.

PARISH MAGAZINES, Church Services, Notices, Guild Rules, Club Cards, Rules, etc., neatly and expeditiously printed at the lowest prices. Estimates post free from WARREN'S Works, High-St., Winchester.

THE BUGLE CALL: THE SOLDIERS' MONTHLY. Edited by CHARLES EDWARDS, with illustrations. Crown 4to, 16 pp. 1d. monthly.

HOW TO PRINT AND PUBLISH A BOOK. This handy little Volume also contains information on Printing generally. Price 6d., post free.

LETTERPRESS PRINTING, LITHOGRAPHY, RULING, BOOKBINDING, EMBOSSING, in Best Style at Low Prices. Estimates by Return Post from WARREN'S GENERAL PRINTING WORKS, WINCHESTER.